"Read this book. I have known Dennis Hollinger ... what it is to balance head, heart and hands is not just an academic exercise ... nis. He lives it."

RICHARD L. GATHRO, EXECUTIVE VICE PRESIDENT, COUNCIL FOR CHRISTIAN COLLEGES & UNIVERSITIES

"Dennis Hollinger's book is a gift to the church. With wisdom and care, Hollinger leads us on a journey around the pitfalls of an unbalanced life into the green pastures of healthy living that exercises head, heart and hands. The destination is nothing less than an imitation of Christ."

STEPHEN B. KELLOUGH, CHAPLAIN, WHEATON COLLEGE

"The central thesis of this book is solidly biblical: Every Christian should be bent toward integrating mind, heart and hands—the mental, emotional and practical. Can a book (mental) stir the passions (emotions) and thus lead to action (practice)? I join Dennis Hollinger in hoping it will."

JAMES W. SIRE, AUTHOR OF *THE UNIVERSE NEXT DOOR* AND *HABITS OF THE MIND*

"Dennis Hollinger's book can be summed up in one word: *congruency*. Christians are challenged to live congruent lives. May we heed Hollinger's challenge to live our life with our head, heart and hands."

JOSEPH B. MODICA, UNIVERSITY CHAPLAIN, EASTERN UNIVERSITY

"Dennis Hollinger, in a skillful and succinct way, has covered a lot of ground in this book on such an important topic for Christian discipleship and moral formation. By providing pertinent biblical, theological and historical background on the different emphases on head, heart and hands, along with contemporary theoretical insights and pastoral concerns, Dr. Hollinger reminds us why we need to listen to the whole of the Scriptures, along with Christian tradition, for this important integration of head, heart and hands. This book, with its engaging questions and practical applications, will benefit all readers seeking to wholly love God with heart, mind and soul."

WYNDY CORBIN, ASSOCIATE PROFESSOR OF ETHICS AND THEOLOGY, ASHLAND THEOLOGICAL SEMINARY

"Dennis Hollinger provides wise counsel for correcting a defect that plagues us all these days: the fragmenting of our lives—not only as individuals but also in our congregations and outreach ministries. We desperately need the reintegration of head, heart and hands that he calls for!"

RICHARD J. MOUW, PRESIDENT AND PROFESSOR OF CHRISTIAN PHILOSOPHY, FULLER THEOLOGICAL SEMINARY

"This is an important book, based on a deceptively simple premise: that Christian existence, rightly understood, involves a holistic integration of head, heart and hands. Hollinger's careful exposition of his thesis points out the very many ways in which Christian faith can become unbalanced in the direction of head (mind), heart (emotion) or hands (action), as well as the sometimes disastrous consequences of these various distorted versions of Christianity.

"This book could serve very well as a programmatic foundation for a local church's preaching and teaching ministry or for Christian educational institutions such as our colleges and universities. I predict that *Head, Heart & Hands* will be used with great value in a wide variety of such settings. I recommend this book with enthusiasm."

DAVID P. GUSHEE, GRAVES PROFESSOR OF MORAL PHILOSOPHY, UNION UNIVERSITY

"Anyone who wants to better know, love and serve God and their neighbor will love this book. With skillful insight, Dennis Hollinger guides us into a thoroughly biblical understanding of the holistic relationship between our thoughts, feelings, passions and actions, pointing the way to a deeper intimacy with God and a more Christlike discipleship and witness in today's world. I wish I had read something like this thirty years ago. Highly recommended!"

THOMAS A. TARRANTS III, PRESIDENT, C. S. LEWIS INSTITUTE

"We are all unbalanced, we begin to realize, as Dennis Hollinger unfolds for us the intertwining necessities for faith to be that of head, heart and hands. However, this book does not just diagnose our lopsidedness; it also offers counsel for deepening all aspects of vital and whole faith and for nurturing their mutualities. The result is not just 1 + 1 + 1 = 3, for each dimension in the totality of faith makes the other two more influential. Share this book with other 'unsound' believers."

MARVA J. DAWN, AUTHOR, TEACHING FELLOW IN SPIRITUAL THEOLOGY, REGENT COLLEGE

"This calm, gentle and carefully reasoned book persuasively depicts Christianity as 'a whole faith for the whole person.' Through wise use of Scripture and discerning attention to everyday real life, Dennis Hollinger shows how crucial it is for faithful believers to keep together active use of the mind, deeply ingrained habits of the heart and serious engagement with the world. *Head, Heart & Hands* is an ideal book for promoting a full-orbed Christian faith."

MARK A. NOLL, MCMANIS PROFESSOR OF CHRISTIAN THOUGHT, WHEATON COLLEGE, AND AUTHOR OF *THE SCANDAL OF THE EVANGELICAL MIND*

HEAD, HEART & HANDS

BRINGING TOGETHER

CHRISTIAN THOUGHT,

PASSION AND ACTION

DENNIS P. HOLLINGER

IVP Books
An imprint of InterVarsity Press
Downers Grove, Illinois

InterVarsity Press
P.O. Box 1400, Downers Grove, IL 60515-1426
World Wide Web: www.ivpress.com
E-mail: email@ivpress.com

InterVarsity Press® is the book-publishing division of InterVarsity Christian Fellowship/USA®, a movement of students and faculty active on campus at hundreds of universities, colleges and schools of nursing in the United States of America, and a member movement of the International Fellowship of Evangelical Students. For information about local and regional activities, write Public Relations Dept., InterVarsity Christian Fellowship/USA, 6400 Schroeder Rd., P.O. Box 7895, Madison, WI 53707-7895, or visit the IVCF website at <www.intervarsity.org>.

Scripture quotations, unless otherwise noted, are from the New Revised Standard Version of the Bible, *copyright 1989 by the Division of Christian Education of the National Council of the Churches of Christ in the USA. Used by permission. All rights reserved.*

While all the stories and examples in this book are based on real people and situations, some names and identifying details have been altered to protect the privacy of the individuals involved.

Design: Cindy Kiple
Images: Andrew Penner/iStockphoto

ISBN 978-0-8308-3263-7

Printed in the United States of America ∞

Library of Congress Cataloging-in-Publication Data
Hollinger, Dennis P., 1948-
  Head, heart and hands: bringing together Christian thought,
passion, and action / Dennis P. Hollinger.
      p. cm.
  Includes bibliographical references.
  ISBN 0-8308-3263-7 (pbk.: alk. paper)
  1. Christian life. I. Title.
  BV4501.3.H66 2005
  248—dc22

                                                                              2004029843

P		12	20	19	18	17	16	15	14	13	12	11	10	9	8	7	6	5
Y		25	24	23	22	21	20	19	18	17	16	15	14	13	12	11		

To my parents,

Elam and Gertrude Hollinger,

who taught me to love God with

head, heart and hands.

CONTENTS

PREFACE

It has been more than twenty years since I preached my first sermon on the theme of this book. I well remember the response of one gentleman, who was a leader in a Christian organization. He said to me, "I now understand why my wife and I have always struggled in having devotions together. In retrospect I think she has a faith of the head, and I, a faith of the heart. No wonder it's been so hard for us to really connect."

At that moment I sensed that I was on to something, and that first sermon led to articles, lectures, more sermons, frameworks for ministry goals and evaluation, and now to this book.[1] I am more convinced than ever of its timeliness.

Simply put, I am contending that the head, heart and hands all play a significant role in our Christian faith. Moreover, each dimension plays a vital role in the expression of the others. Our minds, passions and actions interact in such a way that unless all three are present and nurturing each other, we are less than the people God created us to be. To be whole Christians, head, heart and hands must join together as joyous consorts. The problem is that most believers and Christian organizations or movements have accentuated one dimension to the neglect of the others.

In many ways this book reflects my own personal journey and struggles. My natural tendency has been to focus on the mind as the key to Christian faith and experience. My theological education, closest friends and most formative experiences have generally been oriented toward the head. Recognizing the neglect of other dimensions, I pursued a Ph.D. in ethics to give attention to Christian action. In retrospect, it was a focus on action primarily through the lens of thought. And it has always been the need for attending to the heart which is my greatest personal challenge. I am still very much in process in bringing the three together, and I hope this work will be significant for my own personal journey, as well as the journey of the Christian church.

I have attempted to write this book as much as possible in a popular style and language. To the academics: I am acutely aware that there are ongoing debates on many topics surrounding the themes of this work, but this is not the book to pursue those in the language and nuances of the academy. Of particular interest for academics are the questions surrounding the nature of humans and the nature of knowledge. I have attempted, however, to write for as broad an audience as possible, because I believe that the book's theme is so important for all of us attempting to follow Christ, especially in this age.

I am deeply grateful to friends and colleagues who have read and responded to all or parts of the manuscript and offered splendid insights and suggestions. My thanks to the scholars in that group: John Fea (history), Justin Barnard (philosophy) and Mark Senter (Christian education). Milton Gaither (education) and John Addleman (psychology) offered significant ideas and bibliographic suggestions from their respective fields. Thanks to my work-study students—Sarah Wilson, Monique Beadle and Rochelle Yutzy—who helped in reading, making it accessible to college students and even writing some discussion questions. Also, thanks to Provost (now President) Kim Phipps, who granted me some time from teaching to finish this project in my last semester at Messiah College, before assuming the presidency of the Evangelical School of Theology.

It has been a joy to work with the editorial staff at InterVarsity Press. I am particularly appreciative of the work of Al Hsu and the anonymous readers who gave invaluable feedback to the early draft.

As always, my family is important in my writing projects. Kudos go to my daughter Daphne, who, after reading the manuscript, gave her usual hard questions for Dad to ponder. Naphtali and Nathan have listened and responded to ideas from this book over popcorn and iced tea on various occasions. And Mary Ann, my companion and confidante for these many years, has been a continual source of inspiration and support in my writing.

Above all, I wish to thank my parents, Elam and Gertrude Hollinger, who early on in my life helped me understand that faith in Christ involves the whole person—mind, heart and actions. Mother and Dad, for your modeling, prayers, support and love these many years, I say thank you, and dedicate this book to you.

1

FRAGMENTED FAITH
AND FRAGMENTED PEOPLE

Jeff was a thoughtful Christian. He grew up in a secular home that had no time for matters of religion, but during his high school years came to faith in Christ. Because family and friends chided him for his newfound beliefs and commitment, Jeff began to seek answers for the hard questions he faced.

By the time Jeff graduated from a university as a philosophy major, he had developed intellectual rigor regarding Christian beliefs and apologetics. He knew the difficult and skeptical questions to his faith, but read broadly to find answers to the challenges. Jeff often found himself in the middle of intellectual debates with fellow students and had ready answers for them. Christians on campus frequently found help through his philosophical and theological responses to the tough issues. Jeff knew what he believed and why he believed it.

But, interestingly, there were significant elements of true and vital faith that seemed to be missing in Jeff's life. Personal prayer, spiritual disciplines and fellowship with other Christians increasingly became a low priority in his life. At times they were hardly evident. In fact he sometimes showed contempt for the personal piety of other believers, noting their shallow emotionality and lack of theological or philosophical depth. Moreover, in his zeal to defend the faith against skeptics, he sometimes showed a lack of compassion and care for people.

Jeff believed, articulated and defended biblical faith. He had what we might call a *faith of the head*. Unfortunately, that's about where it ended.

Christina was a middle-aged woman with a faith expression very different from Jeff's. For her, biblical faith was not so much about beliefs as about a vibrant inner experience, demonstrated with deep emotion. When she led worship in her home church, she exuded enthusiasm, vitality and spontaneity. Christina *felt* her faith in Christ, and the Holy Spirit was continually speaking to the depth of her being. Passion was the essence of her spirituality, and she particularly cherished the various mystical, emotional experiences through which she was drawn nearer to God.

Christina read the Bible, emphasizing that it was not for knowledge and understanding but for "a spiritual zap," as she termed it. She yearned for the Word to move her heart and she yearned to feel the presence and power of God. When it came to making decisions in life, she relied little on the wisdom of others or on reflection on the situation at hand; she prayed for God's direct, inner direction. She felt the leading of God. The Lord was her personal friend.

But there were aspects of Christina's life that caused some to wonder. At one point she had a very emotional, mystical experience in which she claimed that God was telling her to divorce her husband. When friends in her church raised questions from a biblical standpoint, she responded, "I know what the Bible says, but this is what God has told me to do, and I'm going to do it." God had spoken deeply in her soul, so she said, and the divorce became reality.

Christina had what we might call a *faith of the heart*. It was vibrant and alive at one level, but it never seemed to go beyond the affective or emotional side of life. Her inner passions alone dictated her actions, thinking and relationships.

Jennifer had a kind of faith very different from either Christina's or Jeff's. She had grown up in a home and congregation that prized solid biblical teaching and the practice of personal piety. She went to church several times a week and was soaked in an "indoctrination" of the faith.

When Jennifer went off to college, she was exposed to new ways of thinking and began to react to her own family and church. She didn't reject her faith, but believed it needed a radically different form. For Jennifer, action was what it was all about. She came to believe that most acts of piety were hypocritical forms of religiosity that Jesus had repudiated in his injunctions against the Pharisees. The point was not primarily to understand the faith, and certainly not to feel it emotionally. The whole point of following Jesus was to do it—to embody his teachings and actions.

Acts of justice and compassion were the focus of Jennifer's Christianity. She became involved in various programs and movements of social justice in her community, attempting to address issues of environment, race and poverty. Jennifer was living in the heart of the inner city and wanted to give hands and feet to her beliefs in Jesus.

But, interestingly, there were some missing parts to Jennifer's faith. When back home on one occasion, she confessed to a friend from childhood that she did little to nurture her spirituality. She had minimal time for her local church and most of her reading now focused on social issues. As she put it, "I just don't find theology to be helpful to the causes."

Jennifer's life reflected faith in action. She had what we might call a *faith of the hands*. Her commitments to Jesus were primarily about living out his ways in the hurt, anguish and injustices of this world. But that's pretty much where her faith ended.

Jeff, Christina and Jennifer (perhaps in overstated form) reflect three types of faith: head, heart and hands. Taken alone, these types are deeply flawed and inadequate, for thought, passion and action separated from each other are in conflict with the way God created us. Such a separation is inconsistent with what Jesus demonstrated in his own life. Too often throughout the history of Christianity, these types of faith expression have tended to focus on one dimension and minimize the others. At one level we can perhaps read the whole history of Christianity through this lens of head, heart and hands, as individuals, churches and movements have tended to emphasize one approach, often in reaction to the others.

The Christian faith is rooted in transcendence. That is, our personal faith in Christ, our directives for Christian living from the Bible and our own personal spiritual experiences all have their ultimate foundation from beyond this world. They are grounded in the triune God of the universe and made known through divine revelation. Nonetheless, our faith is experienced, understood and lived out within the framework of a fallen world, in specific cultures and within the limits of our own finite, sinful selves. Thus, as we understand, experience and express this transcendent faith, we do so in ways that to some degree reflect our environment and even our own personalities.

As a result, individual believers, churches and Christian movements frequently accentuate one dimension of faith over others. Thus some of us are somewhat like Jeff as we accentuate the head. Some of us are a bit like Christina as we focus on the heart. And still others of us are a bit like Jennifer as we make the hands our priority. By themselves, none of these orientations can do justice to the rich understandings of biblical faith. Taken alone, thought, passion and action render a fragmented faith that only further engenders a fragmented self and a fragmented church. Isolated from the other dimensions, our mind can never truly be the mind God intended; our affections can never truly be the affections God intended; and our actions can never truly be the actions God intended.

What we need today, in a fragmented world, is a whole faith of the head, heart and hands, with each dimension feeding and sustaining the others. After all, God has created us as whole beings so that the three dimensions are just that—three dimensions of our unified selves. It is in the joyous consort of our whole selves that we begin to experience God's design for our lives. And it is precisely this model that Jesus exemplified in his life and ministry.

But to understand where we need to be and how we get there, it is helpful to explore these types individually. Perhaps we find ourselves or our churches in one of these three expressions. Although few individuals, churches or movements are ever purely of the head, heart or hands, we have a tendency to accentuate one at the expense of the others.

FAITH OF THE HEAD

Many Christians have understood their faith to be primarily a cognitive enterprise. For these folks, Christianity is a set of beliefs, doctrines and ethical understandings—a worldview to which one adheres. In turn this worldview is then the fountainhead of one's feelings and actions. Most faith-of-the-head types do not avoid affections and expressions of witness or mercy, but believe the key to them is the mind.

From the faith of the head perspective, conversion is seen primarily as a transformation of thinking, with old idolatries and commitments giving way to new perspectives. The Christian life is a growth in knowledge, mediated through the Word of God. The primary goal of life is to cognitively know and defend the Christian understanding of reality. Mastery of the Bible and theology are the most important elements in spiritual development.

Underlying a faith of the head is the assumption that the mind, the *ratio,* is the center of human personality, that thinking is the essence of human nature. This approach, therefore, assumes that if we have our thinking straight in beliefs about God, the Bible, salvation, ethics and the like, everything else will fall naturally into place. Jeff, for example, clearly believed that if a person's head was screwed on straight regarding God and his designs, most personal and social problems would be solved. Why? Because the human mind is the key to transforming the inner self, motivating right human action and even impacting the world for Christ. Thus one reads the Bible not to be moved to action or inward affections, but to gain understanding. Worship of this type is primarily cognitive in that the music, liturgy and sermons all focus on mental understandings of divine realities, from which will come a transformation of the will and actions in everyday life.

One recent author, attempting to correct evangelical negligence of the mind, seems to reflect this type. He argues, "That the mind is the crucial component in the spiritual journey cannot be accurately denied." He goes on to contend that "the mind is the soul's primary vehicle for making contact with God, and it plays a fundamental role in the process of human maturation and change, including spiritual transformation."[1]

Adherents to the faith of the head in many ways reflect the famous rationalist dictum of seventeenth-century philosopher René Descartes: "I *think,* therefore I am." Thinking is the seat of our passions, inclinations and behavior. It is the salient feature of our lives and the crucial element in Christian expression. And of course one can seemingly find good biblical affirmation for such an approach:

> Do not be conformed to this world, but be transformed by the renewing of your minds, so that you may discern what is the will of God—what is good and acceptable and perfect. (Rom 12:2)

> Always be ready to make your defense [*apologia,* a reasoned defense] to anyone who demands from you an accounting for the hope that is in you. (1 Pet 3:15)

Christians of this type emphasize that knowledge of Scripture, understanding of theology, a clear grasp of God's designs and even a cognitive grasp of our world are the primary means to Christian faithfulness.

There is a long history of this approach in the Christian church. Often it has appeared in reaction to emotional or activist excesses; sometimes it has emerged in response to the intellectual challenges of the larger world. Here are some examples of faith focused primarily on the mind.

Medieval Scholasticism. Perhaps the clearest example of a faith of the head was the Scholastic movement in the twelfth through fifteenth cen-

turies. Attempting to give precise philosophical and theological definition to Christianity, these theologians understood the faith primarily as
a rational endeavor through which humans could understand the truths
of God. Scholasticism was often practiced in the medieval monasteries,
which were committed to an inner devotional life as well. But many of
the theologians in the movement were primarily oriented toward a faith
of the mind.

The Scholastics are often caricatured as engaging in pointless theological absurdities, such as how many angels can dance on the head of a
pin—a debate that never occurred as far as we know. Scholasticism
"does not refer to a specific system of beliefs, but to a particular way of
organizing theology—a highly developed method of presenting material, making fine distinctions, and attempting to achieve a comprehen-
sive view of theology."[2] Like the medieval mystics, the Scholastics saw
the end or goal of human life as the vision of God. However, they tended
to travel toward this vision primarily through rationality.

Protestant Scholasticism. After the Reformation, Protestants also developed their own Scholasticism in the late sixteenth and seventeenth
centuries. Leaders of the Reformation like Luther and Calvin had given
significant attention to theology and spirituality and to Christian ethics
and action. But many of their followers in the Lutheran and Reformed
strands of the church tended to focus almost exclusively on theology as
they developed "a confessional orthodoxy more strictly defined in its
doctrinal boundaries than the theology of the early Reformers."[3] In the
post-Reformation era these thinkers and many lay people in the church
increasingly identified Christianity primarily "with doctrinal and sacra-
mental correctness."[4] They assumed that orthodoxy was sufficient to
maintain vital Christian thought and life. As a result, Christian piety and
outward expression were sometimes neglected.

Protestant Scholasticism was not restricted to the centuries immediately following the Reformation. For example, in the nineteenth century
Charles Hodge of Princeton Theological Seminary attempted to show

that theology was akin to the natural sciences. He wrote, "The Bible is to the theologian what nature is to the man of science. It is his storehouse of facts; and his method of ascertaining what the Bible teaches, is the same as that which the natural philosopher adapts to ascertain what nature teaches."[5] Aspects of Scholasticism are currently found in some of the confessional movements within Lutheranism and the Reformed tradition.

Liberalism (modernism). A faith of the head, however, has not been limited to theological orthodoxy, for nineteenth- and early-twentieth-century liberalism (or modernism) had one strand that was highly rationalistic in orientation. While some strands of liberalism were more romantic and heart oriented in their accommodation of faith to the modern impulses, others attempted a rational harmonizing of Christian thought to modern ideals in philosophy and the sciences. The common stereotype is that liberals focused on ethics and action, but some were content with a faith of the mind, arguing that classical Christianity must be expressed in new categories that modern humanity could accept. These new categories often minimized transcendence and the supernatural. Reason, without affection or actions, was the primary criterion for these theologians, so that even divine revelation was pushed aside.

Fundamentalism. In reaction to rationalistic, liberal theology (and other strands of modernism as well), parts of fundamentalism in the early twentieth century reflected a faith of the head. While the movement often fostered a strong anti-intellectual stance with regard to knowledge of the world, it had a tendency toward a rationalistic orthodoxy as the key to battling unorthodox theology. Fundamentalist leaders were separatists from the culture and from suspect church leaders and movements, but they assumed that the watershed battles of the faith would be won and lost in the minds, not the hearts or the hands, of people.

Though they had a place for inner piety and missions, the fundamentalists were frequently suspicious of emotional expressions of faith and social ethic engagements within culture. They attempted to construct airtight categories in their theological arguments, with minimal room for deviation on doctrines that historically were deemed secondary to the core of Christian belief.

This head-oriented legacy of fundamentalism deeply impacted later-twentieth-century evangelicalism, at least in some quarters. For example, seminary education usually focused primarily on biblical studies, theology, apologetics and pastoral functions, with virtually no attention to spiritual formation, ethics or cultural context. I have friends who have told me that in their ordination process they were pressed heavily on matters of theology, with little examination of their spiritual state, relational capabilities, leadership qualities or emotionally stability. The assumption seemed to be that right exegesis and theology would take care of everything in ministry and the life of the church. In the contemporary evangelical scene the landscape is far more diverse and fragmented than several decades ago, but many still see the mind as the key to authentic faith.

FAITH OF THE HEART

Advocates for a faith of the heart see Christianity primarily in terms of feelings, passion, affections and deep spiritual experiences. Faith is understood as an inward, mystical or emotional encounter with the living God. In this view, conversion is a shattering of the soul. The believer encounters God in a deeply personal, living, dynamic fashion, so that feelings and inclinations of the heart are forever changed. Christian growth is perceived as an increasing awareness of the presence of God and an unleashing of divine power within. In this manner, one's will is refashioned and one's thinking and actions are brought into line with God's will.

Here one reads the Scriptures much like Christina in the beginning of our chapter, not for cognitive understandings, but to have one's heart warmed and moved by God. Even the interpretation of God's Word often banks more on the immediate, inner directions of the Holy Spirit, with minimal attention to hermeneutical principles that are tested over time by the church. This was evident, for example, among some of the radical

theologians of the Reformation such as Thomas Muntzer and Caspar
Schwenckfeld, who taught that "every individual had the right to inter-
pret scripture as he or she pleased, subject to the guidance of the Holy
Spirit."[6] Worship in this type is primarily emotive, with music, liturgy
and sermon all aiming to move the affections Godward.

The underlying assumption of a faith of the heart is that affection and
emotion are the most significant features of personhood. We are most
truly ourselves in the deepest recesses of our being. The locus of Christian expression is primarily inward, for it is the heart that affects our
mind and our deeds. In this paradigm, Descartes's dictum would be "I
feel, therefore I am." If believers could only have their hearts enflamed
by the power and presence of God, they would be different people, the
church would change and the world would be transformed. As one recent work on spirituality put it, "The nature of the faith to which Jesus
calls and that our times demand is a religion of the heart."[7]

And of course the heart folks can find plenty of biblical ammunition:

> The LORD is my strength and my shield; in him my heart trusts; so I am
> helped, and my heart exults. (Ps 28:7)

> I will give them one heart, and put a new spirit within them; I will remove
> the heart of stone from their flesh and give them a heart of flesh, so that
> they may follow my statutes and keep my ordinances and obey them.
> (Ezek 11:19-20)

> They [the disciples] said to each other, "Were not our hearts burning
> within us while he was talking to us on the road, while he was opening
> the scriptures to us?" (Lk 24:32)

There is a long history of the heart approach to faith in the Christian
church. It has often emerged in response to a cold orthodoxy or an
action-oriented faith that lacked spirituality.

Mysticism. One of the classical examples is mysticism in the medieval
church. Mysticism in general is the inner, spiritual quest for union with
the divine, sought primarily through noncognitive processes, such as the

purging of physical desire, purification of the will and inward illumination. It has often been characterized by a strong anti-institutional demeanor and thus has sometimes been considered highly suspect in the eyes of the institutional church.

In the medieval church, mystics were often at the opposite spectrum from the Scholastics in how they perceived Christian faith and spiritual life. The primary means to experiencing divine realities was not through the mind, but through intuition and an inward absorption of transcendence. The Christian mystics varied significantly in the path to this inward experience and in the perceived relationship between the contemplative life and the active life. However, most agreed that the inner journey to God was to be found primarily in the depths of the inner self. Writing in the midst of various upheavals in medieval culture, such as the Crusades, religious and political conflict, and the plague, the mystics looked away from the external world to the inner world to find new apprehensions of God and the human condition.

The mystical absorption of God from within is well captured by the Spanish mystic Saint Teresa of Avila: "One sees nothing, either within or without, but while seeing nothing the soul understands quite clearly who it is and where it is and sometimes even what he means to tell it. How and by what means it understands it does not know."[8] Most mystics denigrated the body and rational thought in favor of the soul's direct absorption of God's presence and ways. As one anonymous British mystic put it, "All the time we are living in this mortal body, the clarity of our perception of spiritual matters is always distorted by some kind of illusion, and this applies particularly to our ideas about God."[9] Some mystics emphasized the active life flowing from the contemplative life and most did assume a theology, but the movement was clearly a faith of the heart in its starting point and primary focus.

Pietism. Another faith of the heart movement was Pietism in the seventeenth and eighteenth centuries. Beginning in Germany with leaders such as Philipp Spener and August Francke, Pietism was a reaction against Lutheran Scholasticism and its perceived cold intellectualism and dead orthodoxy. Whereas Luther, and particularly the Protestant Scholastics, had emphasized the more objective side of salvation, the Pietists emphasized the subjective side, with its focus on personal repentance and faith, growth in personal holiness and a daily appropriation of God's grace within. For the early Pietist leaders "the true criteria of authentic Christianity were orthopathy (right feelings) and orthopraxy (right living) along with orthodoxy (right believing)." But they also argued that "right experience and right living would inevitably lead to right believing."[10]

Historians give different renderings on the importance of the mind for the Pietists, but clearly the heart had priority. For the most part they gave significant attention to the active life, embodying both evangelism and deeds of compassion. The movement was particularly known for its *collegia pietatis* (gatherings of piety), in which the followers, usually while remaining in the state church, gathered in small groups for accountability, enabling each other to develop a heart-oriented faith.

Johann Arndt, often revered as the precursor of Pietism with his widely read book *True Christianity,* portrayed the sentiments of many in the movement: "This is true repentance when the heart internally through sorrow and regret is broken down, destroyed, laid low, and by faith and forgiveness of sin is made holy, consoled, purified, changed and made better so that an external improvement in life follows."[11] Most Pietists believed that the orthodoxies of the day simply could not engender that kind of inner, personalized faith. Their impact was significant, helping to give rise to John Wesley and the Methodists, revivalism, holiness movements and a host of free-church movements that emerged in subsequent centuries.

Pentecostal/charismatic movements. A more recent example of a faith of the heart is the Pentecostal/charismatic movement of the past century. Pentecostalism usually refers to the earlier phase of charismatic expression (early twentieth century) as well as the continuing emphasis in denominations that began in that era. Charismatic (sometimes called neo-charismatic) usually refers to more recent expressions outside those traditional Pentecostal denominations, including unlikely places such as the Roman Catholic and Anglican/Episcopalian churches. Both strands focus on "the empowering charisms or gifts of the Spirit and the nurturing fruit of the Spirit. This Spirit-empowered way of living addresses the deep yearning for the immediacy of God's presence among his people."[12]

The modern Pentecostal movement began in the early part of the twentieth century with Holiness preachers such as Charles Parham and W. J. Seymour. Seymour, an African American, was barred from a black church in Los Angeles because of his emphasis on a Pentecostal experience similar to that of the early church in the book of Acts. Early followers began to speak in tongues accompanied by unusual displays of spiritual power, and their message and experiences began to circulate throughout the world. In the early days of Pentecostalism there was an unprecedented racial integration, which unfortunately soon gave way to the racial segregation of the times. The movement spawned numerous denominations, had a significant missionary zeal, but was sometimes wracked by theological controversies, most notably over the doctrine of the Trinity.

By the 1960s the Pentecostal experience was moving beyond the traditional denominations and was influencing mainline Protestant and Roman Catholic bodies. Today the Pentecostal and charismatic movements constitute the second-largest family of Christian churches (following Roman Catholicism) and are the fastest growing religious movements in the world, with 250 million adherents.

Above all, the Pentecostal and charismatic movements stress an immediate, spontaneous leading and empowerment of God, most visible through a "baptism of the Holy Spirit" and speaking in tongues. Adherents are by no means of one mind in all theological matters, even pertaining to these most notable features. But they all stress the inward work of the Spirit as the key to outward expressions. As one executive of a Pentecostal denomination put it, "The unknown tongue is not the stammering of excited vocal organs, but rather the clear utterances of spiritual ecstasy. When the Spirit speaks through you, it will be exalted praise or convicting exhortation." And as another leader put it, "When we speak in tongues, we communicate directly from our spirit to God."[13]

These movements emphasize that the gifts of the Spirit are not confined to the apostolic age and are essential to the life and mission of the church. Along with *glossolalia* (tongues) are gifts of healing, prophecy, discerning the spirits and words of knowledge and wisdom. Spontaneity is highly valued, for it demonstrates the immediate leading of God within the spirit of a human being. Thus, as one writer describes the more traditional Pentecostal style:

> The fundamental precept of Pentecostal worship was that the Holy Spirit alone should direct the order and conduct of a service. Prepared speeches, rehearsal and formality were censured as hindrances to the free operation of the Spirit. Often no speaker would be designated beforehand—with the expectation that the Holy Spirit would make the appointment at the proper time. Sermons were to be delivered extemporaneously as well, as the Spirit—not the note cards—gave the utterance.[14]

In segments of the movements today, such spontaneity is sometimes balanced by emphasis on preparation and education, but clearly the Pentecostal and charismatic movements are the most visible contemporary expression of a faith of the heart. They have had an impact on the wider church, particularly in the current "praise and worship" movement, with its emphasis on passion, spontaneity and the immediacy of God's presence.

FAITH OF THE HANDS

In contrast to emphasizing the mind or the heart, advocates for a faith of the hands stress that the pivotal element in Christian experience is action—it is a faith of doing. Christianity at its core is not about beliefs, doctrines, mystical experiences or inward feelings, though these all may have their place. Rather, the essence of true faith is an outward expression of divine realities, particularly in witness, service, justice and acts of mercy. While faith is a decision of the will, it is demonstrated as an outward reflection of the living Christ. It is a lived faith, in contrast to a believed or felt faith.

In this type of faith expression, conversion is exchanging an old way of life for new patterns of existence within the world. Faith must be lived, or it is not genuine faith. Christian growth is most evident not in what one believes or in what one feels, but in actions. The most salient mechanism for ensuring maturity is actions in the human body, for people grow by doing.

A faith of the hands does not deny the head and the heart but emphasizes that human action is the starting point in Christian responsibility and the most significant sign of a genuine relationship with God. Moreover, it is the catalyst for personal beliefs and inward sentiments, and thus has a way of actually developing and nurturing Christian faith. Witnessing to one's faith in Christ is not primarily a matter of right theology but of actual practice. Justice and mercy are not learned in a workshop or classroom, but are carved into the human heart and made habits of one's being through getting into the rough and tumble of the real world. In the process of doing, according to faith-of-the-hands proponents, hearts are curiously transformed and thinking is solidified.

The underlying assumption of this approach is that the essence of human nature is *homo faber,* the person as doer or maker. What distinguishes us from other creatures in the world is our ability to choose and to act in meaningful ways. God grants us the ability and task of caring for the world, and we are most human in carrying out that stewardly task. In this perspective, action is the lens into the human soul and the best evidence of our worldview. Because actions best exemplify our humanness, the dictum would be, "I *act,* therefore I am."

Of course there is much biblical warrant for a faith of the hands:

For we are what he has made us, created in Christ Jesus for good works, which God prepared beforehand to be our way of life. (Eph 2:10)

What good is it, my brothers and sisters, if you say you have faith but do not have works? Can faith save you? If a brother or sister is naked and lacks daily food, and one of you says to them, "Go in peace; keep warm and eat your fill," and yet you do not supply their bodily needs, what is the good of that? So faith by itself, if it has no works, is dead. (Jas 2:14-17)

Go therefore and make disciples of all nations, baptizing them in the name of the Father and of the Son and of the Holy Spirit, and teaching them to obey everything that I have commanded you. (Mt 28:19-20)

Throughout the history of the church, this type has been manifest in two main subgroups: those who emphasize *proclamation* of the gospel (evangelism) and those who emphasize *presence* (actions of mercy, justice and service). Some have managed to keep these two domains of word and deed together, but often they have been distinct or polarized agendas in the church's mission to the world. Both, however, represent an activist faith of doing.

Ministries of proclamation. The emphasis on proclaiming the gospel of Jesus Christ is one of the expressions of a faith of the hands. For this strand, the most important task in life is to tell others the good news of Christ's death and resurrection for human sin and to invite them to salvation.

This form of activism is readily seen in parts of the modern mission movement beginning in the eighteenth century and reaching its apex in the later part of the nineteenth century. "When in 1792 a self-educated teacher, shoemaker and pastor wrote *An Enquiry into the Obligations of Christians to Use Means for the Conversion of the Heathens,* an utter explosion of missionary zeal resulted, and the 'means' that he wrote about stimulated the founding of countless mission societies."[15] This book became the catalyst and guide for the modern mission movement, and through it William Carey came to be known as the "Father of Protestant

Missions." Carey had a vision that the gospel must be preached to the ends of the earth, for obedience to the Great Commission was at the heart of responsibility to God. Despite the protests of church leaders, Carey went to India and his example became an impetus for thousands who would follow his example in the next two centuries.

The modern mission movement was not without its theologians and those who attended to inward spirituality, but many who heeded the call agreed with Carey that the most important task in the world is proclaiming the gospel to those who had never heard it.

A faith of the hands through proclamation or word has also been evident in many evangelists of the past several centuries. One of the best known was Dwight L. Moody (1837-1899). Moody was converted in Boston at age seventeen while working in his uncle's shoe store. He moved to Chicago and became a very successful shoe salesman, while simultaneously beginning to minister in the Chicago slums. Eventually Moody began to preach, and in the last several decades of the 1800s he drew enormous crowds in England, Scotland and Ireland, as well as the major cities throughout the United States.

Moody never had formal theological training and tended to be skeptical of theological education. He was an activist who brought new strategies of management into his evangelistic campaigns. For Moody there was too little time to debate theological minutiae or await mystical visions; the priority task of evangelism was to be done now. Moody said, "I look on this world as a wrecked vessel. God has given men a life-boat, and said to me, 'Moody, save all you can.' . . . This world is getting darker and darker; its ruin is coming nearer and nearer. If you have any friends in this wreck unsaved, you had better not lose time in getting them off."[16] Such was a faith of the hands with a powerful impact on an activist, pragmatic evangelicalism of the nineteenth century.

Ministries of presence. The second form of a faith of the hands stresses Christian presence—actions of mercy, justice and service, particularly addressing the social and physical needs of humanity and the structural arrangements of society. Throughout Christian history, ministries of presence have been evident in a variety of people and movements.

One of the best-known adherents to a faith of the hands was Saint Francis of Assisi in Italy during the early thirteenth century. Francis grew up in the home of a wealthy merchant and lived a carefree life, void of spiritual commitments. Through imprisonment and illness Francis had a life-changing encounter with God that eventually led him to a ministry of preaching and charity, characterized by a life of simplicity. He devoted much of his life to leading a small group of followers who cared for the outcasts and lepers of society. A faith of the hands was so important to Francis of Assisi that he purportedly encouraged his followers to "preach the gospel at all times, and if necessary use words."

The Anabaptist movement is another expression of a faith of the hands through presence. At the time of the Reformation some leaders wanted to push the Reformation further with emphasis on a believer's church marked by adult baptism, discipleship, service and a rejection of the use of violence. These radical reformers were often called Anabaptists (that is, Rebaptizers), and today the movement is best evidenced in the Mennonite churches. While piety and evangelism have sometimes been marks of Anabaptism, the primary focus has been service toward both those within and those outside the church. In the past half-century some strands of Anabaptism have moved beyond acts of mercy to emphasize justice and peacemaking within the larger society.

One of the most influential examples of a faith of the hands was the social gospel movement in the late nineteenth and early twentieth centuries. In the midst of sweeping social and cultural changes, a number of theologians and pastors began to apply the teachings of Jesus to the social realities around them, most notably the economic world. At the heart of their teaching was a belief that the kingdom of God (understood as a set of principles embodied in and taught by Jesus) could become a possibility within history. The social gospelers emphasized that God not only wants to save individuals (an emphasis that was often neglected in the movement), but also wants to transform social structures.

One of the best-known theologians of the social gospel movement was Walter Rauschenbusch, a Baptist minister who pastored in Hell's Kitchen on New York City's West Side. He was more orthodox theologically than many of his cohorts, but was a staunch defender of the idea that the kingdom of God meant human action, change and progress in society. For Rauschenbusch, "Christianizing the social order means bringing it into harmony with the ethical convictions which we identify with Christ."[17]

While some of the social gospelers gave moderate attention to matters of the mind, matters of the heart were frequently minimized. The gospel was primarily about a kingdom that could reshape the patterns of society. The leaders of the social gospel movement were not Utopian, "but their estimate of human potential was consistently high so that in most cases they believed humans could be guided to make the right choices and so contribute to the 'building of the kingdom.'"[18] Clearly the social gospel movement was a faith of the hands.

A more recent rendition is liberation theology, which flourished in the last several decades of the twentieth century. Emerging in the context of Latin American poverty and oppression, a theology based on the exodus (that is, liberation) motif of the Old Testament began to be articulated by a number of Roman Catholic theologians. Drawing on Marxist social analysis, liberationists emphasized that God was on the side of the poor and oppressed in a unique way, and thus any valid faith must join in that identification and quest for social liberation. Eventually the movement spread to other parts of the world and church traditions, and was applied not only to economic realities, but also to issues of race and gender.

Liberation theology is not only a mandate for social change; it is also a new method for doing theology. The starting point of this theology is praxis, a unity of theory and practice in the concrete situations of society. One does not begin theology by reflecting on the Bible, God, salvation or the kingdom, but rather by confronting the realities of this world, most notably social oppression.

Liberation theologians have clearly given attention to the mind, for they write theologies, and some have even articulated spiritualities for liberation. Nonetheless, both the starting point and the goal of liberationists is a faith of action. Gustavo Gutiérrez, who wrote what many perceive to be the most significant theology of the movement, contends that while social liberation does not exhaust the full meaning of Christian faith or salvation, it must always be a foundational element. He believes that the goal of any theology is "a profound transformation, a social revolution, which will radically and qualitatively change the conditions in which they now live."[19]

A WHOLE FAITH FOR THE WHOLE PERSON

Faith expressions dominated primarily by the head, the heart or the hands have been the norm throughout much of Christian history. Most individual Christians, churches and movements have tended to accentuate one element over the others. Many of the individuals and movements just discussed have made significant contributions to the life of our faith, for which we give thanks. From them we have gleaned new understandings, practices and emphases. But taken alone, a faith of the head, heart or hands is deeply flawed, for each represents a fragmented faith with imbalances and inadequacies that we ought not to replicate.

What is needed in our time (as is true for all times) is a whole faith for the whole person. Thought, passion and action need to be present in our lives and in the life of any church or movement. But there is more to the story. Not only do we need attention to the mind, affections and actions, but we also should allow them to nurture each other. When they join in symphonic concert together, we recognize that the head, heart and hands are not three distinct parts, but three interacting dimensions of our whole being.

In this book I am not attempting just to argue that we need theology (the head), spirituality (the heart) and mission (the hands). Such a portrayal misses the depth and significance of what I am attempting, and would continue in many ways to segment the three dimensions.

Rather, what I invite us to consider is that the head, heart and hands need each other in the sense that they nurture each other, and each is integral to the expression of the others. We get our Christian heads on straight not merely by thinking good thoughts, but also by hearts attuned to God and in actions that reflect the glory and purposes of God. We develop sensitive hearts to the Lord not just by powerful inward experiences, but by solid biblical and theological thinking and actions that themselves cultivate our passions. And we engender actions of witness, justice and mercy not merely by our efforts, but by a profound spirituality of the heart and by a biblical and theological thinking that can guide and sustain our steps. While each of us may have a natural tendency toward one emphasis, we need to bring head, heart and hands together in mutual reinforcement. Then we are able to reflect a whole faith of the whole person.

In the rest of this book I seek to show how this might be so. In the next few chapters we will explore the head, heart and hands biblically and theologically, looking at the role they each play in authentic Christian faith. We will also see what happens when we underplay or overplay each element. In the final chapters we will see the ways in which biblical faith brings the three together in splendid harmony, with implications for Christian living in a fragmented, postmodern world. We will also explore the challenges we face in holding thought, passion and action together.

Jeff, Christina and Jennifer each seem at first glance to represent a vital and committed faith in Christ. But each reflects a fragmentation that fails to do justice to the way God created them and to the designs God has for them. Each needs to begin a transformative journey into a more harmonious, integrated whole. This is the great need of their lives and ours, as we follow Christ in a fragmented but seeking world.

DISCUSSION QUESTIONS

1. Have you met any Jeffs, Christinas or Jennifers in your faith experi-

ence? What did you admire about their understandings or expressions of Christianity? What seemed to be lacking?

2. What factors do you think may have contributed to the faith expressions of Jeff, Christina and Jennifer? How can we as Christians be aware of those factors in influencing our own expression of faith in Christ?

3. Which of the three types of faith (head, heart, hands) do you most identify with? Least identify with? How have you come to develop this faith expression?

4. How do you think we might be able to overcome the fragmented faith that separates head, heart and hands? How might churches and Christian organizations seek to overcome this separation?

2

CHRISTIAN FAITH
AND THE HEAD

Christians have often been ambivalent about the human mind. For some it has been the primary avenue to Christian truth, conversion, spiritual maturity and engagement with the world. For others it has been the great enemy of the soul, the surest path to abandoning one's faith or acquiescence to a fallen world.

I recall, for example, a sermon I heard in college, calling students to use their minds for Christ. As this Christian leader put it, "Only when we have transformed our way of thinking and enabled others through Christ to transform their patterns of thought can we ever begin to transform our world for the sake of God's kingdom." The mind was heralded as the key to our mission to the world.

But I also recall a student's question to me one day in a seminary ethics class I was teaching—a question that puzzled me at first. He asked, "Is intellectual inquiry ethical?" I probed a bit regarding what he was after. He pointed out that when Adam and Eve fell in the garden, the whole issue seemed to focus on knowledge: "When you eat of it your eyes will be opened, and you will be like God, knowing good and evil"

(Gen 3:5). This student feared that the pursuits of the mind, particularly apart from divine revelation and the promptings of the Spirit, could lead us astray. He believed that this was the lesson to be learned from the Garden of Eden.

Many of us come from church backgrounds where the mind has been denigrated. As Mark Noll, a church historian at Wheaton College, once put it, "The scandal of the evangelical mind is that there is not much of an evangelical mind." Noll commends this wing of Christendom for its sacrifices in spreading the good news of Christ, its openhearted generosity to the poor and its countless hours of voluntary giving to the church and Christian organizations. But he also laments that "modern American evangelicals have failed notably in sustaining serious intellectual life."[1]

The irony in Noll's apt description is that many of these same Christians have, in part, been a people of the head. They have believed that the mind is the primary means by which spiritual growth takes place and the primary vehicle through which we worship our Lord and carry out his mission in the world. But they have been skeptical of using the mind to engage the larger world. Thus, clearly these believers have had a selective use of the mind. As an acquaintance of mine said to a friend on hearing that I was headed off to do Ph.D. studies, "He needs that like a hole in the head." This gentleman was certain that intellectual pursuits would lead me astray. Numerous believers come from church traditions that carry these suspicions.

So as followers of Christ, how do we view the mind? What role does it play in the Christian life? These are the questions we will probe in this chapter.

THE ROLE OF THE HEAD IN THE BIBLE

The ancient Greek philosopher Aristotle once said, "All men by nature have a desire to know."[2] He did not acknowledge the source of this innate drive, but from a biblical viewpoint it stems from our creation in the image of God. Just as God is the ultimate source of all knowledge and wisdom, and reveals knowledge, wisdom and direction to us, so we reflect his image in the use of our minds. This is the starting point for a biblical understanding of the head, and as we will see, there is much throughout the Bible that supports the crucial role of thinking in all of life.

In the Garden of Eden we find that God communicates with Adam and Eve in a way that he does not with animals. Adam and Eve were granted not only the task of caring for the good world into which they were placed, but also the opportunity to name and to classify the animal world. Our first human parents also were expected to be able to discern morally and spiritually. All of these things are functions of the mind and reflect a creation in God's image. Though the human race fell into sin and human thinking was marred and distorted, we continue to reflect the image of God by our ability to think. The very capacity we have to reason, imagine, classify, recall, symbolize and compare is a result of that creation in which we are set apart from the rest of the created world.

The fact that God has taken the initiative to reveal himself and his ways to us presupposes the use of the head. God's self-disclosure comes to us both through his magnificent creation (general revelation) and through his more specific disclosure in the written Word, the Bible, and the incarnate Word, Christ (special revelation). God's creation, with its beauty and intricacies, not only stirs our hearts with a sense of awe, wonder and aesthetic appreciation but also speaks to our minds. Thus the psalmist could exude, "The heavens are telling the glory of God; / and the firmament proclaims his handiwork. / Day to day pours forth speech, / and night to night declares knowledge. / There is no speech, nor are there words; / their voice is not heard; / yet their voice goes out through all the earth, / and their words to the end of the world" (Ps 19:1-4).

Because God has spoken through his creation, we are responsible for that knowledge. In Romans 1 and 2 the apostle Paul explains that both the reality of God and at least some of his ways are known through the handiwork of our Creator. "Ever since the creation of the world his eternal power and divine nature, invisible though they are, have been understood and seen through the things he has made. So [people] are without excuse" (1:20). Even people who do not have the law or special revelation of God often "do instinctively what the law requires. . . . They show that what the law requires is written on their hearts, to which their own conscience also bears witness" (2:14-15).

Christians have long debated how much we can know of God and his designs through creation, and the degree to which we can bank on human reason as part of that created order. But the very fact that God has spoken in this manner and holds humanity accountable for this general revelation presupposes the significance of the mind. Moreover, God's creation and our divine calling to tend that creation remind us of the grandeur of our cognitive capacities. The whole world, because it is God's world, is open before us to explore, examine and describe. As a result we can, in the words of the famous astronomer Johannes Kepler, "think God's thoughts after him."[3]

When it comes to special revelation in Christ and the Bible, knowledge of God and his ways is made explicit. The fact that God has directly spoken in word and in person tells us two things: that our minds matter and that we grasp reality (including divine reality) in multiple ways.

When we think about the head component, we may tend to think of logic, clear reasoning, systematic investigation or perhaps linear forms of thought. When we begin to explore God's Word, we of course find some of those styles of cognition. But the Bible unfolds with multiple forms and genres: narrative, history, letters, poetry, parables, speeches, systematic argument and apocalyptic imagery. This alone should tell us that God has endowed us with multiple forms of thought.

Scientists who study the brain describe two sides (or hemispheres) of this splendid organ. The left lobe of the brain tends to be linked to the more linear, systematic and classifying aspects of our thinking. We usually learn math, logic and sequential thinking with the left hemisphere. The right brain focuses more on images, symbols, intuitions and aesthetic forms of thinking. It tends to be more relational, intuitive and feeling-oriented as it processes reality. No one is ever purely "right brained" or "left brained," but we often have a propensity in one direction over the other. The very fact that God has spoken in multiple ways to us affirms all forms of cognition, when understood with reference to our Maker. Thus both the logician and the artist reflect the image of God.

But what exactly does the head do when it comes to our Christian lives? What specific role does it play? Scripture points to at least three areas in which we see the importance of thinking: conversion, Christian growth and maturity, and engagement with the world.

Conversion. Though we are created with a capacity to think, one of the first things we find in the pages of Scripture is that our thinking has gone awry. In our fallen condition our natural knowledge of and yearning for God turns us to false gods, establishes false perceptions of the world and allows us to use knowledge in evil ways. Thus this good gift of God has become darkened. In the story of the Fall in Genesis 3, the man and the woman pridefully decided that they wanted a knowledge beyond their finite limitations and in autonomy from their Maker. The problem is not knowledge but an autonomous knowledge on their own terms, apart from God.

God intervenes to restore us to himself through the death and resurrection of Jesus Christ. When we respond to him in faith, there is a turning within ourselves, through God's initiative and enablement, back toward God's designs. In both the process and effects of conversion, the head plays a vital role. The word for repentance in the New Testament (*metanoia*) literally means to change one's mind, and this is a salient part of conversion. Of course conversion always involves more than the mind, but without the mind there is no true conversion.

In Romans 10 Paul gave significant insight into the process of a person's coming to faith in Christ, a process that always involves both head and heart: "If you confess with your lips that Jesus is Lord and believe in your heart that God raised him from the dead, you will be saved" (v. 9). The confession with the lips clearly involves a public declaration and a cognitive dimension. It is not merely a feeling one has about Christ or even a will to follow him in life. There is certain content that is embraced—"Jesus is Lord." To affirm cognitively that Jesus is Lord doesn't bring salvation, but without it there is no salvation.

The commitment to Jesus as Savior and Lord carries with it other beliefs. One theologian put it this way: "He who with his whole heart believes in Jesus as the son of God is thereby committed to much else besides. He is committed to a view of God, to a view of man, to a view of sin, to a view of redemption, to a view of human destiny, found only in Christianity."[4]

We must be careful not to add more than is warranted in this cognitive affirmation, as Christians have sometimes done. Coming to faith in Christ is not dependent on affirming a particular system of theology, beliefs about matters such as baptism or the return of Christ, or our favorite theological hobbyhorse and language. But despite the potential for theological misuses, there must be some clear understandings about Jesus, God and humanity. The early Christian apostles believed that the gospel included a message that was to be received and held to firmly through our cognitive faculties (1 Cor 15:1-2). The crux of this message was "that Christ died for our sins in accordance with the scriptures, and that he was buried, and that he was raised on the third day" (1 Cor 15:3-4).

Of course the gospel of Jesus is evidenced by more than mere words. Our lives of consistent character, enduring love, uncompromising justice and personal holiness are a message about the reality of a loving, forgiving God who wants all to come to him. And yet this gospel must be demonstrated by more than action and character. It is to be spoken and proclaimed—acts involving cognition. Paul in Romans 10 asked how any will believe unless they have heard the good news and how any will hear unless someone proclaims (vv. 14-15). "So faith comes from what is heard, and what is heard comes through the word of Christ" (v. 17).

Thus there is content to the gospel. One cannot believe in pantheism (the belief that everything is God) or in polytheism (the belief in many gods) and embrace the one triune God of the Bible through faith in Christ. Likewise, a person cannot believe that Jesus was merely a great human and have saving faith. Such cognitive commitments are incompatible with what the Bible teaches is necessary to affirm in order to know God and experience divine redemption.

Christian life and maturity. Just as the head plays a role in coming to Christ, so too it plays a vital role in growing in grace and living out the life of Christ. There are many people who, as the Scriptures put it, "have a zeal for God, but it is not enlightened" (Rom 10:2). Having great spiritual experiences that stir our emotions will not necessarily engender spiritual depth and maturity.

Christian growth is an experience in growing closer to the living God and thereby being transformed into divine likeness. A key element in that transformative process is our thinking: "Do not be conformed to this world, but be transformed by the renewing of your minds, so that you may discern what is the will of God—what is good and acceptable and perfect" (Rom 12:2). Certainly we will be disappointed if we think this transformation and growth comes only by understanding more of the Bible or having greater insights of theology. That is not what Paul is teaching. The renewing of our minds will never be a purely cognitive enterprise.

On the other hand we will not have transformed minds unless we are attentive to biblically informed thought. A significant part of this transformation is what goes into our minds. If we fill our minds with things that dishonor God, others and self (that is, sin), we will reap negative results in our affections and actions. If we fill our minds with the good things of God, mediated through his Word, we will reap a "harvest of righteousness" (Phil 1:11) in all dimensions of life.

According to Scripture our growth toward maturity involves teaching and understanding. As the Lord, speaking through the psalmist, says, "I will instruct you and teach you the way you should go; / I will counsel you with my eye upon you. / Do not be like a horse or a mule, without understanding, / whose temper must be curbed with bit and bridle, / else

it will not stay near you" (32:8-9). The teachings of God, through both
his Word and through the church's accumulated wisdom, serve to keep
us near Christ and hence to embody his ways in life.

Thought is important not only because God's designs must be known
if we are to live them and inwardly experience them, but also because the
mind motivates and sustains us in living those designs. Numerous biblical texts teach the importance of knowledge for growth and maturity:

> We have not ceased praying for you and asking that you may be filled
> with the knowledge of God's will in all spiritual wisdom and understand-
> ing, so that you may lead lives worthy of the Lord. (Col 1:9-10)

> So if you have been raised with Christ, seek the things that are above,
> where Christ is seated at the right hand of God. Set your minds on things
> that are above. (Col 3:1-2)

> . . . the new self, which is being renewed in knowledge according to the
> image of its creator. (Col 3:10)

> You were taught to put away your former way of life, your old self, corrupt
> and deluded by its lusts, and to be renewed in the spirit of your minds.
> (Eph 4:22-23)

> And this is my prayer, that your love may overflow more and more with
> knowledge and full insight to help you to determine what is best. (Phil
> 1:9-10)

> Finally, beloved, whatever is true, whatever is honorable, whatever is just,
> whatever is pure, whatever is pleasing, whatever is commendable, if there
> is any excellence and if there is anything worthy of praise, think about
> these things. (Phil 4:8)

There is sometimes a tendency to think of spirituality and Christian
growth as primarily an inward reality, a matter of the heart. But these
texts remind us that the mind plays a key role as well. With the mind we
understand something of the triune God we follow in life. With the mind
we understand the patterns, designs, virtues and key spiritual disciplines
that go into the spiritual growth process. And with the mind there is an

actual direction and empowerment toward that process. Because ideas have consequences, the head clearly is vital to the Christian life, as it impacts both the affectional and behavioral dimensions of life.

Even the spiritual disciplines we utilize to encourage spirituality and maturity cannot lay aside the mind. Take prayer, for example. Clearly we pray with our hearts, the inner affection of our being, and in so doing we often feel close to God. There is even a role for a type of prayer that does not focus on knowledge or ideas—that is, praying in the spirit. But the apostle Paul also reminds us, "If I pray in a tongue, my spirit prays but my mind is unproductive. What should I do then? I will pray with the spirit, but I will pray with the mind also; I will sing praise with the spirit, but I will sing praise with the mind also" (1 Cor 14:14-15). Even our spiritual disciplines that focus most specifically on our inward selves (that is, the heart) can never be divorced from our minds and the role of cognitive understandings.

Engagement with the world. As we engage the world around us we must do so with the guidance and perspectives of the head. As we will see in chapter six ("Christian Faith and the Hands"), our involvement within the world embodies two dimensions: presence and proclamation. Presence is the involvement with our lives, character and actions; Christians are called to live in the world with a new pattern of life that reflects the kingdom of God, which was most visibly inaugurated in the first coming of Christ and will be consummated in his second coming. Proclamation is the verbal articulation of the meaning of Christ and his kingdom. Both play a significant role in our mission to the world, and in both dimensions the mind is vital.

Christian presence within the world requires clear understanding of the moral virtues and norms that God desires from his creatures. Without such understanding, we have little sense of God's direction for our lives, the church and society. For followers of Christ, these virtues and norms reflect the patterns of our Lord and Savior and the standards of his kingdom. We employ the mind as we seek to discern these virtues and norms from the Bible and from the life of Christ. Justice, love, integrity, righteousness, purity of heart, respect for human dignity and compassion for the disenfranchised are standards that we must come to understand as well as incorporate into the core of our being. Living these out in the midst of a complex world is no simple task, especially as we seek to apply them to aspects of public life such as business, economics, politics, education, the environment and culture.

It is one thing to attempt to understand these God-given designs for humanity; it is quite another to apply them in the push and pull of a secular, pluralistic world. Application of biblical norms calls for wise discernment that reflects an understanding of both the biblical standards themselves and the world into which we apply them. Our norms and virtues are transcendent and absolute; our strategies in applying them are humanly devised and relative, calling for an understanding of the issues, the context and the potential impact of our strategies (or technical solutions) for the ethical and social problems we face.

Take the familiar words of Micah 6:8, which are so important in engaging our world: "And what does the LORD require of you / but to do justice, and to love kindness, / and to walk humbly with your God?" Understanding the nature of justice and love from within a Christian perspective is a starting point. But then we must go on to think about the strategies of justice and love in issues like poverty, race relations, abortion and political life. In our search for appropriate venues to implement our Christian convictions, we need solid research on the issues themselves and analysis of how our strategies will impact both the society and ourselves. Without the use of the mind in these efforts, we will fall prey to mere ideological thinking that brings minimal Christian perspective to the issues we face.

The other part of our engagement with the world is proclamation, the verbal telling of the good news of Christ. Here too the head is essential. One of the best examples of this is the ways the apostle Paul proclaimed the gospel in the various contexts in which he ministered, as narrated in the book of Acts. When Paul was preaching and teaching in Jewish settings, he employed the language, stories and images of the Hebrew people from the Old Testament. He attempted to show how Christ fulfilled all that the prophets spoke of and longed for in the coming Messiah. He employed cultural and religious analysis to understand his own people and the ways the gospel would make sense to them. But when Paul went to the Gentiles, his language and appeals changed. For example, in Paul's encounter with the Epicurean and Stoic philosophers in Athens, he shows that he has done rigorous cultural, philosophical, literary and religious analysis to understand the context of his listeners and hence to contextualize the Christian message. He makes no use of the Hebrew Scriptures, as they were foreign to the Athenians. Instead he appeals to Athenian writers and thinkers to show how Jesus fulfills their philosophical and religious quests: "Athenians, I see how extremely religious you are in every way. For as I went through the city and looked carefully at the objects of your worship, I found among them an altar with the inscription, 'To an unknown god.' What therefore you worship as unknown, this I proclaim to you" (Acts 17:22-23).

Paul then goes on to quote from their writers and philosophers as he proclaims that the God they seek can only truly be found through "a man whom [God] has appointed, and of this he has given assurance to all by raising him from the dead" (Acts 17:31).

Christians have sometimes denigrated the mind in proclaiming the gospel by appealing to texts like 1 Corinthians 1: "For the message of the cross is foolishness to those who are perishing. . . . Where is the one who is wise? . . . Where is the debater of this age? Has not God made foolish the wisdom of the world?" (vv. 18, 20). Or they have noted Paul's caution to "see to it that no one takes you captive through philosophy and empty deceit, according to human tradition" (Col 2:8). We must recognize, however, that Paul is not denigrating reason per se, but rather an autonomous reason that pushes God aside from the knowing process. The very fact that Paul, other biblical writers and Jesus utilized reason and

argumentation in their writings and discourses evidences the importance of disciplined thinking.

The New Testament further tells believers that they are to engage the
ideas of the world around them. In a passage acknowledging that spiritual warfare involves ideas, Paul stated, "We destroy arguments and every proud obstacle raised up against the knowledge of God, and we take
every thought captive to obey Christ" (2 Cor 10:4-5). Peter challenged
believers to "always be ready to make your defense [apologia, from which
we get the word apologetics] to anyone who demands from you an ac-
counting for the hope that is in you; yet do it with gentleness and reverence" (1 Pet 3:15-16). This implies a well-thought-through response to
the questions that inevitably emerge regarding our faith.

These texts do not mean that all human ideas or intellectual paradigms are antithetical to our commitment to Christ. But because all
forms of knowledge ultimately rest on some prior conceptions or worldview assumptions, there will at times be conflicts. To engage the world,
we must then understand the thought of the world, affirming where we
can affirm and critiquing where assumptions and ideas are at odds with
a Christian worldview and biblical understandings.

THE CONTENTS OF THE HEAD: A CHRISTIAN WORLDVIEW

Whenever human beings think, it is not isolated thoughts or a garnering
of facts and data apart from a larger context. Our thinking (as well as our
affections and actions) is always situated in a larger worldview framework through which we make sense of everyday reality. Our worldview
is essentially the way we put our world together. It involves our perceptions of ultimate reality (that is, God), an account of what is wrong
within the world, a portrayal of how to deal with that wrong, an assess-
ment of human nature in relation to the rest of nature and a rendition of
where history is headed. Our worldview may not always be consciously
held and may at times lack coherence, but it is integral to who we are
and how we daily transact our lives.

Understanding a Christian worldview is vital for grasping the significance of the mind, but also for understanding the Bible and our faith. We best understand the particulars of our Christian faith by grasping the larger biblical narrative, which forms the heart of a biblical worldview. For example, the death and resurrection of Jesus Christ only make sense in light of the larger story about God, our selves and the meaning of salvation. A friend once told me that the first few times she heard the gospel it made absolutely no sense to her. She couldn't figure out how a man who lived two thousand years ago and died on a cross could possibly have any relevance to her life. It was only when she began to hear the whole story of a God who created humanity and of a world that is fallen from its original design that the death and resurrection of Christ began to make sense.

We only begin to grasp the meaning of a Christian ethic in light of our larger worldview perceptions about God, humanity, the world, salvation and the course of human history. As David Naugle has pointed out, "Since nothing could be of greater importance than the way human beings understand God, themselves, the cosmos, and their place in it, it is not surprising that a worldview warfare is at the heart of the conflict between the powers of good and evil."[5]

In the previous section we attempted to show that the head is important in the Bible as evidenced in conversion, spiritual growth and engagement with the world. But now we seek to go further in an attempt to understand the important cognitive content of our faith. It is this worldview content—the broad overarching strokes of the biblical story—that serves as the framework for understanding specific biblical texts and the particular doctrines of Christian faith. Our worldview is essentially our theology in its most foundational form, and it significantly impacts our heart and our hands. As we will see later, our heart and hands also impact our worldview.

Despite the diversity of biblical interpretations and theological beliefs throughout Christian history, there is, I believe, a core to our faith; what

C. S. Lewis often called "mere Christianity." Essentially the biblical narrative or Christian worldview can be summarized in four parts: creation, Fall, redemption and consummation. This is the heart of the biblical drama, and it forms the essence of our Christian worldview. All interpretations of Scripture and all renditions of particular doctrines (the Trinity, the nature of Christ, the meaning of Christ's atonement, etc.) are best understood in light of this bigger picture.

Our worldview is, of course, derived from the Bible, God's written Word, but it is derived through a process of analyzing the pivotal events, significant contours and overall shape of the biblical message. Without such worldview understanding, our faith will be shallow and easily captivated by the cultural mood. Without the big-picture worldview of creation, Fall, redemption and consummation, the Bible will seem like a jumble of teachings and stories unrelated to each other or to life. In perceiving this worldview we see both the importance of thinking and the essential content of Christian thought.

Creation. When believers reflect on creation, they sometimes become embroiled in how God did it, when it occurred or the degree to which God may have utilized natural processes (which were, of course, divinely established) in carrying out his creation. In these debates it is easy to lose the worldview significance of creation.

At the heart of a biblical view of creation is the story of a good God creating a good world, with human beings at the apex of God's creation. Such an account differs from a number of other worldviews. For example, some cultures and religions have viewed creation as the result of a battle between the forces of good and evil. Others have perceived creation as an endless cycle of birth, death and rebirth. Still others have seen creation as a purely mechanistic enterprise understood entirely through the processes of nature. Our worldview about creation is not only a matter of understanding our world and ourselves; it powerfully impacts the way we live.

In the biblical story, God creates a good world. The physical "stuff" of the universe (that is, material reality) is said to be good, for after the particular days of creation, "God saw that it was good." After God created human beings in his own image and looked at the entirety of his created world, "God saw everything that he had made, and indeed, it was very good" (Gen 1:31).

The goodness of creation stands in stark contrast to many worldviews in which the material dimensions of the world and human life are seen as problematic at best and evil at worst. For example, in New Testament times there were some schools of philosophy, drawing on and reinterpreting the tradition of Plato, which believed that because matter was essentially evil, the incarnation—God coming in human flesh—was impossible. In fact fairly early in the Christian church some began to teach that Jesus did not have a physical body, but only seemed to have one. The heresy of Docetism, as it was called, was clearly at odds with the biblical portrayals. John, for example, went out of his way to describe the empirical and material reality of Jesus in the flesh in contrast to Docetism: "We declare to you what was from the beginning, what we have heard, what we have seen with our eyes, what we have looked at and touched with our hands, concerning the word of life" (1 Jn 1:1).

What are the implications of this part of the biblical worldview, that the world in its material form is created good? For one thing, it implies that the universe God made is a place where we can work, investigate, study and live our lives. God doesn't call us away from the world to some "soulish" place, but calls us to live in the midst of this physical universe and the cultures therein. Thus the calling of a scientist to investigate and describe the universe is a true Christian vocation, a calling from God.

The goodness of creation means that many of the gifts to the human race are wonderful gifts of our Maker. Take the gift of sex. Contrary to the way some through the centuries have perceived physical intimacy, the most important thing that can be said about this dimension of our humanness is that it is a good gift of our Creator. As a good gift, it finds its true meaning within divinely ordained purposes, namely, the consummation of a marriage (that is, one flesh), procreation, expression of love and pleasure. These purposes come together in the marriage of a man and a woman and thus provide the boundaries for experiencing the marvelous gift of creation.

Whenever humans see the material world as inherently evil or problematic, they tend to fall prey to ascetic understandings and experiences of sexuality that denigrate its goodness. But the biblical concept of creation teaches otherwise. In its rebuttal of false teachers, 1 Timothy says, "They forbid marriage and demand abstinence from foods, which God created to be received with thanksgiving by those who believe and know the truth. For everything created by God is good, and nothing is to be rejected, provided it is received with thanksgiving" (4:3-4).

I have frequently spoken on this subject to young people and college students, and usually begin by asking the question, "When you hear the word *sex*, what comes to your mind?" Among Christians I find that the responses are sometimes negative. Many have failed to grasp the goodness of this gift, and thus their thinking and often their actions are distorted.

Another aspect of the biblical worldview from creation is that human beings are specially made, and thus set apart from the rest of the created order:

> So God created humankind in his image, in the image of God he created them; male and female he created them. God blessed them, and God said to them, "Be fruitful and multiply, and fill the earth and subdue it; and have dominion over the fish of the sea and over the birds of the air and over every living thing that moves on the earth." (Gen 1:27-28)

One of the most significant aspects of our identity is that we bear God's image. Thus we are different from the rest of creation. Jesus clearly affirmed this distinctiveness when, in upholding the value of a sheep who needs our care, he said, "How much more valuable is a human being than a sheep!" (Mt 12:12). In the creation story of Genesis, part of the image is demonstrated in the human stewardship and care for the rest of creation, which is distinct from the man and the woman and under their God-appointed dominion.

Being made in God's image also means that we are relational beings, reflecting the relational dimension that exists within the triune Godhead. Thus, whenever we enter into good friendships, including the friendship of marriage, we are demonstrating the *imago Dei*. Because humans bear God's image, they have a value and dignity that is not dependent on how much they are valued by others, how well they function or what contribution they make to society. Our worth and dignity simply is, because we bear that divine image. Such dignity carries with it important consideration for a host of contemporary ethical issues ranging from bioethics, to race relations, to life in the workplace. Human uniqueness and sanctity are to be preserved in every phase of life from conception to death. Indeed how we think about human beings has considerable impact on how we treat them.

The Fall. Though God created a good world with humans at the apex of his creation, it is quite obvious that the world and human life are not as God intended. In fact it is sometimes said that the Fall and human sin is the one Christian doctrine that is empirically verifiable. Everywhere we see its menacing effects.

All worldviews embody both some sense of human nature and a portrayal of the fundamental problem in human life and the universe. Some worldviews have been very positive about human nature, believing that if we have sufficient education, harness our scientific and technological know-how and develop positive structures in society, we can achieve a good and just social order. The Enlightenment worldview, which so significantly impacted the modern world from the eighteenth through twentieth centuries, carried this assumption about life. As Francis Fukuyama of Johns Hopkins University points out, "Beginning with the French Revolution, the world has been convulsed with a series of Utopian political movements that sought to create earthly heaven by radically rearranging the most basic institutions of society, from the family to private property to the state."[6] But rather than heaven on earth, these Utopian dreams created havoc and human degradation.

On the other hand, some worldviews have been extremely pessimistic about human nature, believing that society must place significant external restraints on human behavior, usually through a state accentuating order. This type of worldview sees human beings as almost bestial and can be seen in thinkers like Machiavelli in the fifteenth and sixteenth centuries and Thomas Hobbes in the seventeenth. Within this perspective is a radical distrust of humans and little sense that human dignity and rights must be protected. This type of thinking has tended to lead to totalitarian political structures.

In contrast to these assumptions, the Christian worldview affirms that humans are created as good creatures who bear the image of God and thus possess an intrinsic dignity. But simultaneously it affirms that humans are fallen creatures who destroy God's designs, seek their own autonomy apart from God and live their lives with reference to their own interests rather than to the interests of God and neighbor. Biblical faith holds together these two assumptions.

The story of the Fall in Genesis 3 most explicitly states what went wrong with God's good creation. Moreover, it is a portrayal of our fallen patterns today, best understood in terms of four alienations: from God, others, self and nature. In the Christian perception of reality, the heart of human and societal problems ultimately stems from sin. Of course this does not discount other factors that influence human character and behavior, such as psychological, sociological, biological, economic, political and historical realities. But underneath all ailments in the world is an understanding of our fallen condition and our rebellion against our Maker and his designs. Sin affects not only people, but also cultures and societies, and the institutions within them.

The nature of the fallen condition means that Christians ought to be suspicious of Utopian social schemes or political agendas that do not take account of this fundamental malady. This understanding should not lead to an utter pessimism or to complacency in attempting to address the many personal and societal problems in our world. But in the Christian worldview, there will always be a recognition that even the best human and institutional efforts at goodness and justice are still inflicted with pride, self-sufficiency and attempts to place ourselves over the good of others and the glory of God.

I recall a conversation I had one day with a congressional chief of staff while I was pastoring in Washington, D.C. He mentioned to me that he always found that he had more in common with fellow Christians on "the other side of the aisle" than with nonbelievers in his own political party. "With fellow Christians we share common assumptions about the nature of human beings," he said, "and that makes a huge difference. Though a person may have a different political viewpoint, such a difference is about strategy, such as the size and role of government. But sharing fundamental worldview assumptions brings us closer together than a person in my political party whose essential worldview is at odds with my own." In my time in the nation's capital I often witnessed deep friendships between Christians in opposing political parties. One of the key elements in these friendships was a shared worldview, including a common view of humanity.

The Christian worldview teaches us that we are wonderfully made, but terribly fallen. It is this unique understanding that ought to guide our perception of self, others and society, and our behavior relative to these domains.

Redemption. Though the human race is badly fallen from God's original designs, the story fortunately does not end in despair. As soon as humankind turns against its Maker, he begins a process to draw his creatures back to himself and to heal the breach that has infected every dimension of human life, culture and the natural world. In the Christian worldview, this redemption does not reside with human capabilities, but is initiated and effected by God's own grace and redeeming actions, through the death and resurrection of his Son, Jesus Christ.

Every worldview has some notion of "salvation," a portrayal of how to right the world's wrongs. In the Enlightenment worldview, salvation comes through education and knowledge; in Marxism, through an economic revolution; in some Eastern religions, through a process of ascetic self-control and rebirth; and in postmodernity, through an acceptance of the belief that there are no ultimate and universal solutions—only relative and local ones. In each of these worldviews, redemption depends on the initiative and ingenuity of human beings or on the inevitable forces of history. But in the Christian worldview, redemption is not dependent on ourselves, for "if anyone is in Christ, there is a new creation: everything old has passed away; see everything has become new! All this is from God" (2 Cor 5:17-18).

This Christian solution to the cosmic wreckage does not, however, reject all human efforts at coping within our fallen state or trying to better this sinful world. Believers should affirm that God in his common grace has granted good gifts to the human race which all can utilize in their attempts to find their way in a broken world. Because God has bestowed these gifts and his created order is good, humans apart from God's saving grace have some glimpse of his truth and can avail themselves of these good gifts: medicine, psychology, education, social work, family, human government, business, the arts and so on. These are all partial means of coping with our fallenness and brokenness.

The problem comes when people turn these gifts into gods, expecting from them more than they can yield and thus falling prey to an idolatry that distorts the ultimate meaning of life. Gifts of common grace in their proper place should be affirmed by Christians. But they are not the ultimate solution to the human predicament, for that is found in Christ alone.

This cognitive understanding and commitment significantly impacts how we live and how we approach the world around us. The reconciliation and forgiveness we know through Christ is the foundation and motivation for demonstrating reconciliation and forgiveness to those around us. Salvation does not remove us from the realities of the world, but sends us back into the world as agents of redemption and reconciliation.

Consummation. Though Christ brought redemption and hope to the world through his death and resurrection, it is quite evident that the remnants of the Fall still hold sway. Redemption certainly makes one right before God (justification) and begins a process of renewal, but the realities of sin and brokenness are obvious in the world and in human lives. Even believers who have come to Christ in faith still struggle with the menacing affects of sin, for as Paul lamented, "I do not do the good I want" (Rom 7:19).

In the Christian worldview, this gap between the present realities and the promise of full redemption are understood in light of a final consummation, when God's kingdom becomes a full reality and all things are made new. Thus Christians have a particular view of history, one that sees history moving to a climax with the second coming of Jesus Christ.

Most worldviews have some kind of eschatology, or view of where history is headed and what the end will be. In some worldviews, history is moving toward some type of Utopia, driven by revolutions or changes in the patterns of society. For other worldviews, history moves in a cyclical fashion with no movement toward a climax. And in still other worldviews, history is moving downward to an inevitable collapse, and perhaps even annihilation. These worldview assumptions have inevitable consequences in society and culture, as well as in the lives of people.

In the Christian view of things, there is hope and purpose in history. Because there is a creation, a disrupting Fall and a redeeming initiative, there is a final goal toward which history is moving, under the sovereign reign of God. Some believers throughout history have viewed eschatology (theology of the end) as an escape from the realities of a mixed-up, evil world. But both a closer and bigger-picture reading of Scripture gives a very different vantage point. The consummation with the return of Christ is a source of hope and a motivation for living now in the light of his coming kingdom. Moreover, we are called to reflect that coming kingdom of peace, justice, righteousness and love in every dimension of life and in all corners of society (Rom 13:11-14).

The Christian worldview of creation, Fall, redemption and consummation carries cognitive content that directs the course of all our thinking, impacts the sentiments of our hearts and shapes the contours of our actions. As we will see later, the heart and the hands impact our worldview and all cognitive perceptions. But at this point we must recognize the crucial role that the head and worldviews play in life. Worldviews make a difference, and the distinctive elements of a Christian worldview have a powerful impact on individual and corporate life. They do so because the mind matters.

DISCUSSION QUESTIONS

1. Many Christians have assumed that the most important way to use the mind is through the study of the Bible and theology. Does this chapter agree or disagree with that assumption? What are your own understandings about that assumption?

2. Describe in your own words the role of the mind for conversion, Christian growth and engagement with the world. What role has your own mind played in each of these elements of the Christian life? What changes do you envision for your thinking after reading this chapter?

3. How would you describe your own worldview? How does it fit with the worldview described in this chapter: creation, Fall, redemption and consummation?

4. What difference does the worldview of creation, Fall, redemption and consummation make in our personal lives? In society? What do you see as the most pressing issues in our culture, relative to this worldview?

3

DISTORTIONS OF THE HEAD

In the opening chapter we met Christina, a middle-aged woman who neglected Christian thinking, as she experienced her faith primarily through the heart. Christina read the Bible not for guidance in her mind, but for feelings deep within. She justified her divorce primarily on the grounds that God had told her to do so. When friends and fellow church people reminded her of what Scripture taught on the subject and suggested other possibilities for coping with a difficult situation, Christina appealed to God's inward leading for her decision.

Christina represents a distortion of the head, for in her imbalanced emphasis on the heart, she gave minimal attention to the role of the mind. As a result she led a very fragmented life in which her passions frequently were not guided by an external standard from God's Word or from the discernment of fellow believers. Moreover, Christina gave virtually no attention to relating her Christianity to the needs and issues in the world around her. She lived her life primarily with reference to her inward affections. At times she even scorned those who emphasized theological knowledge and understanding.

In that same chapter we met Jeff. He too represented a distortion of the head, though in a different way than Christina. Jeff believed that theology and apologetics would essentially encompass the primary responsibilities of his life as a Christian. He believed that if he got his thinking straight about God, the Bible, Jesus and ethics, everything else would fall into place. Because the mind was to him the key to human existence, right thinking was the key to successfully living and vital faith. Thus his primary focus in life was to understand the Bible, theology, moral obligations, the challenges to Christian belief and a response to those challenges.

Both Christina and Jeff reflect distortions of the head—the one from neglect, the other from overemphasis. In this chapter we explore what happens when these kinds of distortions appear. In conclusion we will examine ways we can avoid such distortions by nurturing the mind for the glory of God.

WHEN THOUGHT IS NEGLECTED

What happens if the mind is neglected in Christian thought and life? What does a faith with minimal thinking produce? What are the implications for the kind of Christianity that Christina exhibits? The consequences are profound.

Incomplete faith. If Christ calls us to love God with our mind (Mt 22:37), then to love without our mind will be an incomplete faith. A faith without the mind tends to be shallow and ill-equipped to cope with the inevitable realities and hard questions of life. Headless Christians usually resort to a faith dominated by feelings alone and become spiritually dependent on their own emotional state or on a series of peak "spiritual experiences," which they seek to continually replicate. Because God is perceived, in this approach, to speak only within, there is no work and guidance of God external to one's own self.

Such a person reflects what Jesus had in mind in the parable of the seeds: "As for what was sown on rocky ground, this is the one who hears the word and immediately receives it with joy; yet such a person has no root, but endures only for a while, and when trouble or persecution arises on account of the word, that person immediately falls away" (Mt 13:20-21). Without the mind, faith will not be sustained, for it will lack a compass, a grounded worldview and the motivations and sustaining guidance necessary for facing life's challenges and disappointments.

By neglecting to love God with the mind, one not only neglects a very crucial dimension of oneself, one also neglects a crucial dimension of God. If God has spoken to us in ways that involve the mind, whether through general revelation or special revelation, to neglect this dimension of God's action is to neglect a salient dimension of God. We will not experience the wholeness that God intends for our lives without the mind, because God has created us to experience himself and his world utilizing the mind.

What does it mean to love God with our minds? It doesn't just mean that we need to think biblically or theologically. It means that we so love God that we will explore his created world and seek to understand his creatures through a Godlike perspective. It means that we will sense the grandeur of God when we use our minds to reflect on our faith, the world and everyday experiences. To love God with our minds means that we will reflect on the good gifts of creation that we experience daily and see God in them: family, neighbors, medicine, sexual intimacy, education, work, leisure, sports, hobbies and the arts. Loving God with our minds accentuates a divine perspective for our thinking, and makes us daily aware that such perspectives come from the hand of God. Thus, to ignore the mind in the Christian life is to fail in our love for God.

Unorthodox faith. A Christianity that disparages the mind also tends to breed heterodox formulations—beliefs that are clearly incongruent with the Bible and a Christian worldview. Unorthodox theological beliefs can easily emerge when there is a failure to use the intellect in understanding God's Word and in grasping the wisdom of the church's historical understandings.

Mark Noll notes that a good example of this can be seen in the Albigenses (or Cathari as they were also labeled) of the Middle Ages. The movement began as a protest against moral laxity in the church, but "their history illustrates how easy it is for Christian groups that undervalue the mind to lapse into the employment of non-Christian thinking." Though they attempted to keep themselves unspotted from the world, the Albigenses intentionally denigrated the life of the mind. As a result they came to embrace a belief that "matter itself was suspect. Redemption meant freeing the spirit from the Body. . . . Christ could never have taken on an actual body of flesh; the kingdom of God must be an utterly ethereal thing, not something that begins in the day-to-day life of each believer."[1]

At the heart of the Cathar theology was a radical dualism of two Gods, one evil and the other good. It taught that the "Good God has no involvement in the material world, as it is tragic, brutal, and wicked. . . . The Evil God created and rules over this world, albeit he is a fallen angel and less powerful than the Good God."[2] Salvation is gained by repudiating the material world and its evil. This is a sharp departure from the biblical worldview (outlined in the last chapter) with its portrayal of evil resulting from the Fall of a good creation and redemption coming from the incarnate Son and his death and real resurrection—all doctrines rejected by this movement. The Albigenses, with their distortions of Scripture, are an illustration of what can easily happen when people negate the significance of solid, in-depth thinking.

Throughout history a number of groups have minimized the use of the mind, fearing it would lead them astray. In reality it was their very rejection of thought that led them astray. For example, in the early days of the Pentecostal movement (early twentieth century) there were some churches and leaders that so denigrated theology that they ended up rejecting one of the most central doctrines of the Christian faith—the Trinity. The "Jesus Only Pentecostals" were unitarians of the second person, believing that the name of the Father, Son and Spirit is Jesus. Their anti-intellectualism could not come to terms with affirmations that demanded the best of biblical and theological scholarship. Their anticreedalism gave no place for the rich tradition of thoughtful Christians throughout the ages.

Today we frequently have theological aberrations not because of anti-intellectualism, but because emotions, personal practices and social ideologies are given priority over good, hard thinking. The uniqueness of Jesus as the only way to God is sometimes questioned, not because of biblical exegesis or even intellectual scrutiny, but because our feelings from being in a pluralistic context breed such views. Similarly, theologies of sex that back away from the traditional Christian stance frequently emerge out of personal and emotional reactions or out of the norms and practices of society, not out of intellectual rigor. Whenever the mind is denigrated, unorthodoxy is sure to follow. This is particularly a temptation of a postmodern ethos that questions rationality as merely a ploy of the powerful. In such a context, Christian thought can easily succumb to a theology of feelings, cultural sentiments and political correctness.

Inability to engage the world. A faith that denigrates the mind will also lack the ability to engage the world in such a way that the church is truly salt and light within it. In their encounter with the world, "thoughtless" Christians tend toward two major distortions: acquiescence to the ideologies of the world, or simplistic, naive attempts to control the world. The acquiescence to the ideologies of the world has been amply demonstrated in both conservative and liberal Christianity by their embracing of politicized attempts at social concern—attempts that look no different from either the conservative wing of the Republican party or the liberal wing of the Democratic party. Many conservative evangelicals so identify with the conservative Republican agenda that it's hard to tell what is uniquely Christian in their thinking. And many mainline or "liberal" Christians so identify with the liberal Democratic agenda that one wonders what happened to biblical thinking. On both sides, solid Christian worldview reflection is missing, and nothing unique is contributed to the social milieu.

Similarly, in their engagement with the world some Christians have naively assumed that they could control the processes of history by simplistically applying biblical ideals or the teachings of Jesus to political and social institutions. They have lacked a thorough understanding of the nature of sin within the world and the nature of redemption in relationship to that world. Moreover, this approach has been naive in its sociological understandings of the world's complexity and of how Christ and culture fit together. Such efforts usually end up with a faith that is controlled by the world in its attempts to control the world.

When the head is neglected, Christian engagement with culture and society most notably suffers from an inability to discern. Without cognitive reflection, there is a tendency to view the world in either-or categories, unable to recognize and sort through the complexity of reality. Thus it will be difficult to view culture in such a way that one can discern those elements that are compatible with Christian faith, those that are clearly incompatible and those that are somewhere in between.

In the fifth century Saint Augustine gave a helpful way of thinking about the discernment of culture, as he employed the story from Exodus 12 of the Hebrew people appropriating Egyptian gold and silver for their own services, despite the way these elements had been used previously. He said,

> If those . . . who are called philosophers happen to have said anything that is true, and agreeable to our faith, . . . not only should we not be afraid of them, but we should even claim back for our own use what they have said. . . . While the heathen certainly have counterfeit and superstitious fictions in all their teachings, . . . which everyone of us must abominate and shun as we go forth from the company of the heathen under the leadership of Christ, their teachings also contain liberal disciplines which are more suited to the service of the truth, as well as a number of most useful ethical principles.[3]

A faith that neglects the mind will lack such discernment and will not be able to perceive and utilize truth that is found beyond the explicit scope of special revelation.

WHEN THOUGHT IS SUPREME

Just as it is possible to have a faith expression that minimizes thought, so it is possible to traverse toward a head-only kind of faith. As we saw in chapter one, there have been various individuals and movements throughout Christian history that have understood the faith primarily in terms of the mind. Like Jeff, they have rightly understood the role that the mind plays in life in general as well as in Christian experience. But they have failed to give adequate attention to the heart and the hands. What happens when thought is supreme to the neglect of other dimensions?

Cold, dead orthodoxy. One of the most obvious results historically is the emergence of a cold orthodoxy that fails to give attention to human affection and actions. Numerous movements of the heart and the hands (that is, mysticism, Pietism, the modern missions movement) were reactions against a cold and lifeless intellectualism that failed to do justice to the whole person and the whole faith. With such cold orthodoxy, faith becomes primarily a set of propositions to which one gives mental assent. The crucial responsibility of a Christian, in this perspective, is to understand, propagate and defend the truth of biblical faith.

In a lopsided faith focusing primarily on the head, one's relationship with God lacks inner vitality, spontaneity and a sense of divine presence. God is easily relegated to a doctrine to be defended or a propositional truth to be understood. The personal nature of God is easily lost, resulting in a failure to experience God in a personal or relational manner. God is worshiped and followed more as a set of ideas than as the personal, living, triune God of the universe, who enters deeply into the core of our being and walks with us through every dimension of life.

Moreover, such a "faith" fails to demonstrate the reality of God in everyday life and in ethical actions. As James put it in his epistle:

> What good is it, my brothers and sisters, if you say you have faith but do not have works? Can [such] faith save you? If a brother or sister is naked and lacks daily food, and one of you says to them, "Go in peace; keep

warm and eat your fill," and yet you do not supply their bodily needs, what is the good of that? So faith by itself, if it has not works, is dead. (2:14-17)

James seems to have in mind here a kind of faith that consists entirely of cognitive assent—faith as a hearer only and not a doer, a stance which James says is self-deceptive (1:22-23).

Self-deception. The self-deception of a faith focused primarily on the mind is often sustained by the false sense of security that beliefs can produce if they are isolated from the other dimensions of the self. Humans often believe tenaciously in ideas as a means of shielding themselves from the ambiguities, questions and complexities of the world. Airtight categories are sometimes devised, not out of a commitment to logical consistency or a love for truth, but out of a sense of insecurity regarding faith, the world and one's self. It is possible to hide behind our cognitive commitments to shield ourselves from the challenges around us or from the tough issues of biblical faith that we inevitably face. But such attempts are self-deceptive, engendering a false sense of security.

In teaching ethics classes I have had ample opportunity to observe how students respond to the complexity of issues that we invariably face. Near the beginning of my courses, I attempt to help students recognize that there is a difference between ethical relativism (no moral absolutes or constants) and moral complexity (varying moral and theological principles at work in a given issue). With complex issues the course of action is not always clear, and we need discernment. There are always students who feel uncomfortable with the notion of complexity, feeling that it is inherently relativistic and inconsistent with claims to absolute truth. As I have attempted to talk personally to these students outside the classroom, I usually find deep insecurities within themselves. Their airtight mental categories and inability to acknowledge complexity is usually a form of self-deception to protect their fragile psyche from the realities of the world about them.

Self-deception may make us feel good about ourselves, but it can distort a proper view of God. We easily begin to create "God" in our own image, so that we can manage the "god" we say we adore and follow. We deceive ourselves by developing a garrison of ideas about God to protect ourselves from the triune God of the universe, who sometimes wants to disturb our own sense of order, propriety, security and peace.

A faith of the head also leads to self-deception in how we perceive ourselves, for as Paul noted, "Knowledge puffs up" (1 Cor 8:1). In my own experience with and observation of people fixated on the mind, there is frequently a sense of self that is immune to the feelings and needs of others. I sense this in others, because I know it was true in my own personal journey. Earlier in life, when I had a hard-core faith of the head, I was often insensitive to the sentiments and needs of other people. My fixation on truth alone and arguments to defend the truth sometimes cut me off from realities in people's lives that may have been preventing them from embracing the truth. I came to realize that part of this self-deception was also intellectual snobbery and spiritual pride, a significant temptation when we focus almost exclusively on thought.

I came to realize that we cannot perceive others' needs and struggles merely through the mind or through some sort of psychological and sociological criterion that reduces a person to statistics. We only begin to truly encounter the other when we feel their own hearts with our heart and begin to engage our whole being (head, heart and hands) within their life experiences. Because I am by nature a person of the head, this remains a constant challenge for me. But I now recognize I will never meet the needs of others by mind alone.

When we focus primarily on the head, we deceive ourselves into believing that once we have articulated and defended the truth, we have performed our Christian obligation. That is why head-only types, in their self-deception, can easily run roughshod over Christians asking doubting questions or unbelievers raising the specter of skepticism. Such doubt and skepticism is rarely purely of the mind. Doubts and questions regarding the Christian faith frequently are related to a broad array of personal experiences, hurts, social contexts and personality tendencies. Such contributing factors to a person's questions and qualms certainly need to be understood through the mind, but they will never be adequately grasped without attention to the heart and the hands. To get inside another person's struggles always demands more than cognitive analysis. Moreover, we have a biblical mandate to make our defense with "gentleness and reverence" (1 Pet 3:16).

Abandonment of faith. While faith-of-the-head types tend to focus on beliefs and thinking as a way of defending and clarifying the faith, such expressions have ironically often contributed to an abandonment of the faith. Adherents to this approach have frequently assumed that right thinking is the surest way to protect the faith and prevent heterodox (unorthodox) formulations. But history shows that those who ardently defended Christianity by mind alone often gave birth to a generation that abandoned Christ. Many of the Enlightenment rationalists and deists were the sons and daughters of seventeenth-century orthodox Scholastics. Many theological liberals in the past century have been the sons and daughters of fundamentalists, who focused on a narrow form of headish Christianity. No doubt some of you reading this are the sons and daughters of dogmatic parents overly fixated on thought and truth. As a result, you may be tempted like those in earlier times to reject orthodox Christianity altogether.

Rudolf Otto, a well-known phenomenologist of religion, gives us some indication as to why orthodox Scholastics produced liberals and skeptics:

> The common dictum that orthodoxy itself has been the mother of rationalism, is in some measure well founded. It is not simply that orthodoxy was preoccupied with doctrine and the framing of dogma, for these have been no less a concern of the wildest mystics. It is rather that orthodoxy found in the construction of dogma and doctrine no way to do justice to the non-rational aspect of its subject. . . . Orthodox Christianity mani-

festly failed to recognize its value, and by this failure gave to the idea of God a one-sidedly intellectualistic and rationalist interpretation.[4]

Thus, when Christians focus on thought alone as a means of defending and protecting the faith, they face the very real prospect of engendering a mindset and heart in which God and transcendence are deemed to be no longer necessary. This should clearly remind us that we cannot live by mind alone.

The inability of the mind alone to grasp the meaning and significance of Christianity is well illustrated by the story of Walker Percy, one of the most penetrating novelists of the twentieth century. Percy had been trained as a physician with a specialization in psychiatry. During his residency, his world was turned upside down when he contracted tuberculosis, putting an end to his medical work. During his five years of recuperation in the midst of the horrors of World War II, Percy began to reflect on the meaning of life. In that search he began to read the Danish philosopher Søren Kierkegaard.

Kierkegaard had noted that "Hegel [the philosopher] had told everything about the world except one thing: what it is to be a man and to live and die." As Percy wrestled with this statement he recognized that "as a scientist I knew so very much about man, but had little idea of what man is."[5] He sensed that in all of his scientific knowledge he had not grasped the moral and spiritual dimensions of human existence. Through his realization that knowledge alone was insufficient, Percy became a Christian believer. He turned to writing and gave us some of the most profound novels for provoking us to wrestle with the ultimate realities of life, morality and spiritual truth. He was able to do so because he knew the importance of the mind, but he also knew that humans cannot live by mind alone.

NURTURING THE MIND

If the mind is so vital to experiencing and living a vibrant Christian life, how do we nurture it? What can sustain a balanced life of the mind that deepens our commitments, sustains our trust in Christ and enables us to live daily for the glory of God? How can we nurture the mind to avoid the distortions we have just noted?

Using the mind: The Bible and theology. It is obvious that the ongoing use of the mind is a key factor in its growth. But what does this look like? Clearly one aspect of nurturing our thinking comes from studying Scripture, Christian worldview issues and theological understandings. All three ingredients need to be on our personal and our churches' menus. We live in a time when biblical literacy in our churches is decreasing, and the reading habits of even Christian leaders are quite thin. Recently a pastor told me with pride that he had not read one theology book since he graduated from seminary twelve years earlier. I shuddered inside, not only for him, but also for the church.

In the study of the Bible we must do far more than a shallow reading for a spiritual high, or a "devotional" reading of the text. Certainly we want God to speak to us through his Word, but God's divine revelation is too important to be treated as just another book for our enjoyment. The authority of Holy Scripture compels us to treat it properly in both its interpretation and its application. Attention to context, the literary genre of the text, the text in relation to what surrounds it and to other texts are all important in understanding and applying the text to our day. Such is essential if we are to move beyond a postmodern hermeneutic of "what speaks to me."

Of course we must be aware of the potential to treat the Bible as merely an academic, abstract textbook, devoid of its power to engage our total lives. This is a very real temptation for Christian college and seminary students. Indeed many seminarians have told me that seminary was a spiritual desert in their own journey with Christ. We need to allow the biblical text to move us to tears (and to laughter) and to grip the core of our being. But it is possible to allow the Word to hold sway personally in our hearts while giving attention to the rigors of biblical interpretation and application that rightly employ the mind.

Studying the Bible quite naturally leads to worldview understandings and implications, as well as to theological study. In using our minds to grasp a Christian worldview and theology, we are not negating the Bible but moving beyond the immediate statements of Scripture to synthesize its teachings and understand the basic assumptions lying behind the text. Worldview and theological studies pull together the overall contours and the main strands of biblical teaching to help us grasp the primary story of life, faith and its implications for everyday existence, as noted in the previous chapter. Worldview analysis and theological reflection involve rigorous cognitive functions, and though they are intimately related to heart and hands, they can never be sustained without the use of the mind. Utilizing the mind for studying God's Word, a Christian worldview and theology nurtures and deepens the mind.

Using the mind: The thought of the world. Nurturing a Christian mind involves more than Bible and theology. We must engage the world of thought around us. The best way to enhance our worldview and theological understandings is by applying them in the world of ideas and the concrete situations of our society. The traditional Christian liberal arts college and university agenda of integrating faith, learning and life must be a commitment of all Christians to some degree. Certainly most believers will not be intellectuals or theologians, and yet we are responsible to nurture the mind in relation to the world of ideas and the contours of our culture.

Thus Christians can grow through both the thoughtful and the popular writings of the culture. Novels, news magazines and newspapers, cultural critiques, historical writings, philosophy, science, the arts, modern psychology and even the most "non-Christian" portrayals of reality ideally ought to be among the fare for Christian readers. We will best develop our Christian worldview and most adequately know how to navigate our way in a secular, pluralistic culture when we understand the times in which we live. Thoughtfully engaging the media world is also important for "taking every thought captive to obey Christ" (2 Cor 10:5).

While much of "reality TV" and current cinema is shallow and morally bankrupt, we will most adequately nurture our Christian thinking when we engage that world through the lens of biblical faith.

There is a tendency among some Christian scholars today to play down the unique contributions Christians can make in the world of thought. Their claim is that the Christian contribution to science, the arts or history is simply to do good science, art and history. There is no unique Christian perspective in intellectual life. Certainly believers should never use their faith as an excuse for shoddy scholarship, shallow thought or inept expression in the arts. But the development of a Christian mind in all disciplines must go alongside a commitment to quality work and to Christian action in relation to the disciplines. Christians are called by God to contribute to the arts, humanities, sciences, social sciences and technical subjects as Christians. And a mature Christianity is one that will engage them with a mind that loves Christ and reflects a Christian worldview in its engagement. Such will solidify our thinking, deepen our faith and bear witness to God's reign in that particular sphere of reality.

Using the mind: The intellectual virtues. In nurturing the mind it is also helpful to think of mental disciplines or what philosopher Jay Wood has called the intellectual virtues.[6] Wood sees four such virtues. First are acquisition virtues, such as inquisitiveness, teachableness and persistence. Second are maintenance virtues, such as analysis, creativity and the ability to defend one's beliefs or views against opposing thought. Third are the communication virtues, such as insight, articulateness and persuasiveness. And finally are the application virtues, such as foresight, problem solving and the ability to implement.

Engendering growth in these intellectual virtues will go a long way in developing Christian minds that God can use for his purposes. These virtues recognize that we think in varying ways and that all thought-forms take discipline. The penetrating critique, honest comparison, creative analysis, aesthetic rendition, empirically based classification and carefully crafted argument are all ways that we can nurture minds that God can use for his glory and the upholding and living of divine truth.

Developing ourselves intellectually as Christians is not just a means toward certain ends, such as evangelism, guarding the faith or growth in understanding, though the mind is essential for these endeavors. Rather, because the mind is a good gift of God, reflecting his image in us, intellectual pursuits have a value in their own right. And part of our divine calling in Christ Jesus our Lord is to develop a God-centered mind for the glory of our Maker, no matter what the mind is examining. As Cardinal John Henry Newman once put it, "All knowledge forms one whole, because its subject-matter is one." Though God is infinitely greater than the world and subject we study, "we cannot truly or fully contemplate it without contemplating Him."[7]

Thus the first and greatest commandment is, "Love the Lord your God with all your heart, and with all your soul, and with all your mind" (Mt 22:37).

DISCUSSION QUESTIONS

1. Describe some of your own encounters with a faith expression that denigrated the mind. Are they similar or different from the characteristics described in this chapter?

2. Describe some of your own encounters with a headish Christianity. Are they similar or different from the characteristics described in this chapter?

3. How did you respond to the assertion that a faith of the head actually leads to an abandonment of the faith? Have you known people who have experienced this?

4. How have you attempted to nurture your mind for the glory of God? What are some of the obstacles you have encountered in doing so?

4

CHRISTIAN FAITH
AND THE HEART

Brennan Manning might seem like an unlikely mentor for Christian consciousness regarding God's love and intimacy with his followers. Manning is a chain-smoking, alcoholic former priest, married and since divorced. He confesses in his writings to "boasting, the inflating of the truth, the pretense of being an intellectual, the impatience with people, and all the times I drank to excess."[1] But through writings, speaking and leading retreats, Manning has been a catalyst for helping others discover the deep, intimate love and presence of God in their lives.

Shortly after a relapse in his struggle with alcohol, this former Franciscan priest went on a retreat to take a deep look at himself and to experience anew the love and presence of God in his life. In that retreat he came to realize that he had largely been unable to *feel* anything since he was eight years old, when a traumatic experience had shut down his memories and feelings. He writes, "The great divorce between my head and my heart endured throughout my ministry. For eighteen years I proclaimed the good news of God's passionate, unconditional love—utterly convicted in my head but not feeling it in my heart. I never felt loved."[2]

Only as Manning stopped living in his head and began to move down into his heart was he able to grasp and experience the grace and forgiveness of God in his life.

Our heart—the deep, inner core of who we are—evokes both joy and apprehension within us. It does so because we recognize that within the heart are inner resources for coping with the challenges of life, but also patterns of affections, feelings, desires and inner thoughts that we alone know and hope to keep that way. The heart is thus both friend and foe. We sense that we need its inner comfort, prodding and restraint. Without attention to the heart, we have no hope of a vibrant, dynamic relationship with Christ. At the same time we also loathe and sometimes fear the heart's insidious longings and its wayward impulses. Thus, without a proper focus within the heart, our relationship with God will be led astray.

In many ways the heart remains a mystery to us. Precisely because it appears to be the source of so much good and so much evil, we experience the heart as a perplexing dimension of ourselves that we can neither fully understand nor totally control. We are often baffled by our own inner desires, passions and feelings. Moreover, at times our heart seems to lead us in ways that conflict with cognitive affirmations. As Blaise Pascal, the seventeenth-century philosopher and mathematician put it, "The heart has its reasons which reason knows nothing of."[3]

In American culture today, there is increased interest in matters of the heart, or what is sometimes called spirituality. While this newfound attention can be good, some interests in the heart can be misguided or even destructive, especially to one's spiritual life. Not all spiritualities are alike from a biblical perspective, for not all spiritual realities are alike. One observer notes:

> A quick tour of the local bookstore will likely display all these proclivities for individualistic questions for something "inner"—inner self, inner child. . . . In the consumerist consciousness of much of the northern

hemisphere, such shopping for a private inner world seems to correspond all too well with the enormous growth of private security firms![4]

Indeed much contemporary fixation on the inner self is a reflection of our insecurities and is focused on making us feel better about ourselves. This search for self-assuredness may have little to do with true spirituality, and in fact often detracts from it.

Thus we need a clear biblical and theological understanding of the heart. When we look to the Bible, we immediately see the significance of this multifaceted inner dimension. The Hebrew and Greek words for our English word *heart* occur well over five hundred times in the Bible. In the book of Proverbs, for example, the heart is the seat of trust (3:5), vigilance (4:23), lust (6:25), deceit (12:20), bitterness (14:10), joy (15:30), discernment (18:15), envy (23:17) and a number of other virtues and vices.

But as followers of Christ, how do we view the heart? What role does it play in the Christian life? These are the issues of this chapter.

WHAT IS THE HEART?

The biblical writers used various terms to describe the inner dimension of human beings. The language of soul, mind, spirit and heart appear frequently in the Bible, usually with reference to the inward facets of a person, though never far removed from the external dimensions, such as the body. Some Christians have attempted to develop a full-fledged "biblical psychology" from these terms, and long debates have ensued as to the relationship of body, mind, soul, spirit and heart. We need to remember, however, that the biblical writers were not attempting to set forth either a systematic theology of the person or a theory of personality in the modern psychological sense. These biblical terms are sometimes used interchangeably and at times have different meanings in different contexts, thus precluding any simplistic system. Moreover, both the Old and New Testaments portray a holistic person in whom the various aspects of human life are integrally related to each other. This stands in contrast to the Western, modern, Enlightenment model, which split apart the mind, heart and body.

As we explore the nature of the heart, we must be careful not to develop airtight, scientific categories to define it. Even in the description that follows, we must be aware that the dimensions of the heart are not isolated parts and that the heart is never far removed from thinking and action. Though we will examine the heart through four dimensions, keep in mind that the human person is a whole being that cannot be carved into several autonomous parts. Even the four dimensions are usually overlapping and interacting, as together they form a basic configuration of our inward self. At the risk of oversimplification, we will seek to understand the heart as will, affections, a pattern of feelings or emotions, and deep-seated thoughts or understandings. Like the head, the heart reflects our creation in the image of God, for God in perfection has will, affections, feelings and understandings.

Will. One dimension of the heart is our inward resolve and determination to act in certain ways. The will is a dimension of our inner being that consciously chooses to act toward certain ends or to refrain from certain activities. This volitional element of the self makes choices and establishes avenues for achieving those choices. The will is more than mere desire, though it may often be accompanied by particular desires. It is the exercise in which we purpose within our hearts some goal and then move in action toward that goal. While we usually think of willing particular actions, we can also will particular thoughts and even emotions.

This dimension of the heart is never far removed from the head. Dallas Willard points out that the will is "dependent in its functioning on the contents of the mind (thoughts, feelings)." But he also notes that "our thoughts and feelings . . . have a crucial dependence on our will, on our choices." Thus "what we think is . . . very much a matter of what we allow ourselves to think, and what we feel is very much a matter of what we allow ourselves to feel."[5]

When the Bible speaks of the heart, oftentimes it has the will primarily in view. For example, Psalm 10:3 speaks of the wicked boasting of "the desires of their heart." Speaking of himself as king, David said, "You have given him his heart's desire, and have not withheld the request of his lips" (Ps 21:2). Speaking of Israel, Paul wrote, "Brothers and sisters, my heart's desire and prayer to God for them is that they may be saved" (Rom 10:1). In an appeal to giving financially to others, 2 Corinthians 9:7 says that people are to give as they have determined in their heart. Peter, taking Simon to task over his desire to gain spiritual power through money, says to the imposter, "Repent therefore of this wickedness of yours, and pray to the Lord that, if possible, the intent of your heart may be forgiven you" (Acts 8:22). Biblical writers speak frequently of people "determining" to act in certain ways, and even if the heart is not mentioned, the contexts usually seem to have the inner self in mind. Thus Hosea says, "My people are bent on turning away from me" (11:7).

Theologians have long debated just how free the human will really is and to what degree the will is dependent on God's direct initiative for human salvation and spiritual growth (that is, sanctification). We know that human volition is never entirely free, for it is enslaved to sin (Rom 6—7), and through its own resolve it is not able to please God. Debates arise over the degree to which the human will is dependent on God's sovereignty and the degree to which it can freely choose to accept God's initiating grace. Though this is not the time and place to further that dialogue, for our purposes we need to note that the will is held accountable for its volitional choices and the actions that flow from them. The will must choose whether to accept God's offer of salvation in Christ and then daily choose to follow or limit God's own righteousness in daily life. Thus a significant dimension of our heart is the will, or our inner resolve to think, feel and act in particular directions.

Affections. Closely related to the will are our affections. This dimension of the heart is focused on the major inclinations of our inward selves by virtue of what we love. Affections are always intertwined with the volitional dimension, but the focus here is less on our resolve to act in a certain way and more on the inward bent or direction of our likes and dislikes. Affections reflect our attachment and devotion to particular objects, persons or ideas. They are our passions in life.

It was Jonathan Edwards, the great eighteenth-century revivalist-theologian-philosopher-pastor, who first gave significant attention to the nature and role of affections in the Christian life. Edwards was writing in the midst of the First Great Awakening, in which thousands of people in New England were experiencing profound and moving encounters with God in salvation and spiritual growth. Because the revival demonstrated itself with fervor and emotion, there were many critics of it, who feared that the heart would overshadow the mind. Edwards responded with several highly developed theological and philosophical responses to the critics, but one of his most lasting and profound was *Religious Affections*. In this work Edwards argued that "true religion, in great part, consists in holy affections,"[6] for without them there is spiritual death.

While Edwards's definition of affections is slightly different from my own, his portrayal is helpful for our insight into the heart. He contended that the human soul is endowed with two faculties: understanding, through which we perceive, judge and discern things; and affections, through which we are inclined or disinclined with respect to the things perceived. He believed that the affections and the will are essentially one, but the affections are the "more vigorous and sensible [relating to the senses] exercises" of the will. That is, our affections are not rational perceptions by which we decide (or will) to do a certain thing, but are inclinations that carry significant feeling and vitality with them. As all aspects of the heart are either "approving and liking, or disapproving and rejecting; so the affections are of two sorts; they are those by which the soul is carried out to what is in view, cleaving to it, or seeking it; or those by which it is averse from it, and opposes it."[7] The bulk of Edwards's work is attempting to discern the "distinguishing signs" of true affections, as opposed to spurious ones, in the context of the Great Awakening.

At times when the Bible speaks of the heart, the focus is on our affections, our deep-seated inclinations that reflect both our loves and our revulsions. For example, speaking through the prophet Ezekiel, the Lord tells the prince of Tyre that judgment is coming "because your heart is proud and you have said, 'I am a god; I sit in the seat of the gods, in the heart of the seas'" (Ezek 28:2). A proud heart with sentiments of divine grandeur reflects the passion of this pagan prince. Throughout the Bible we read of hardened hearts in which God's grace and mercy are rejected by affections of resistance to God. In a more positive vein the psalmist prayed, "As a deer longs for flowing streams, / so my soul longs for you, O God. / My soul thirsts for God, / for the living God. / When shall I come and behold / the face of God?" (42:1-2). In this passage the soul seems to mean essentially the same thing as the heart with its affections, and it indeed plays an important role in spirituality and in worship.

Patterns of feelings or emotions. Feelings or emotions are pleasurable or painful sensations we experience in response to particular events, objects, people or ideas. Some have attempted to differentiate feelings and emotions by defining the latter as more intensified feelings, with passions still more intense than emotions. Others have portrayed emotions as public sensations and feelings as private ones. In a recent work, a neurologist contends that they are a single reality, but "emotions play out in the threats of the body. Feelings play out in the threats of the mind."[8] While there may be some legitimacy to these distinctions, for our purposes we will simply use them interchangeably.

Modern science has discovered that there is a close correlation between our emotions and our bodily states. Emotions are also closely tied to functions of the brain, as the brain sends signals of sensation to the body, as well as the body sending sensations to the brain. Thus a person who is held up by a robber naturally sees threat, which eventually translates into feelings of fear. Similarly, when a basketball player drills a three pointer with the clock winding down to win a championship for his team, the fans and players immediately erupt with emotions of jubilance and joy. These kinds of feelings or emotions are a natural part of life that we experience day in and day out in response to pleasurable or painful stimuli.

The heart, however, is far more than these episodes of emotion. The heart particularly encompasses the more deep-seated patterns of feelings that emerge in relation to the core of who we are. For example, a winning player might experience joy in the moment of triumph, but may not be a particularly joyful person in the pattern of her feelings over the long haul. Everyone to some degree experiences the emotion of anger in the heat of a particular threat to ego, but some people reflect a pattern of anger in the core of their inner being. Thus the heart, as emotions or feelings, reflects overarching patterns of sensation and not just mere episodes of a particular emotion.

When the Bible speaks of the heart, sometimes it is speaking of a pattern of feelings. For example, in Psalm 38 David reflected on his own perils, failures and sins. In the midst of feeling wounded and crushed, he cried out, "My heart throbs, my strength fails me" (v. 10). The Proverbs often point to this dimension of the heart: "Anxiety weighs down the human heart" (12:25); "A cheerful heart is a good medicine, / but a downcast spirit dries up the bones" (17:22). In his zeal and concern for his own people, Paul said, "I have great sorrow and unceasing anguish in my heart" (Rom 9:2). And of course the familiar fruit of the Spirit listing begins with emotional states of the heart: "Love, joy, peace" (Gal 5:22). Love and peace are certainly more than feelings, but in this context they seem to be pointing in the direction of inner states of being.

Feelings or emotions are good gifts of God. God is portrayed in the Bible as a God of emotion, with joy, anger, delight, compassion and sadness. Thus our own emotions are a reflection of our Creator. We should affirm the passionate and emotive side of life as part of our good createdness. But in our fallen state, our emotions also need redemption. Willard wrote, "Feelings are a primary blessing and a primary problem for human life. We cannot live without them and we can hardly live with them. Hence they are also central for spiritual formation in the Christian tradition."[9] This means that, in conjunction with the volitional dimension of the heart, we can change our feelings, and indeed we must if we are to experience a Christlike life. But we cannot ignore them.

Deep-seated thoughts and understanding. It may come as a surprise to think of thoughts and understanding in relation to the heart. They would seem to reside in the head. But close observation of life and study of the Bible show otherwise. For starters, some of the biblical words for *knowing* and *knowledge* convey an inward or experiential kind of knowledge. Knowledge of facts, theories, ideas and events are one kind of knowing, but there is also a knowledge that is closely associated with the sentiments of the heart. For example, the Old Testament word *yada* is not only used for knowing God in a deep and profound way, but also for sexual intimacy between a man and a woman (Gen 4:1; 1 Kings 1:4). Knowing in this sense is personal and experiential in nature and involves far more than the cognitive process.

Even our perceptions of the mind, what we normally think of as the head, are closely intertwined with the heart. C. S. Lewis wrote, "For what you see and hear depends a good deal on where you are standing; it also depends on what sort of person you are."[10] That is, even our worldview perceptions and intellectual commitments are never isolated from the leanings of the heart. What we believe is frequently dependent on what is inside us.

But, beyond the cognitive affirmations that are influenced by the heart, there are also deep-seated forms of knowing and understanding, which are actually dimensions of the heart. In fact at times the biblical words for *heart* are translated "understanding." We may know much about the Bible and the major ideas of Christian theology and still not have this more deeply rooted form of knowing. For example, in recent years a group of biblical scholars, known as the Jesus Seminar, have given themselves to the task of trying to determine what in the gospels is truly from Jesus and what are the whims and wishes of the early church. They have tended to debunk the supernatural Jesus and have ended up with a Jesus who fits their naturalistic sentiments. Not only are their intellectual commitments reflections of the proclivities of their hearts, they are also missing something of the true knowledge and understanding of Jesus and the Bible that comes from a heart that is attuned to God. They may know, but not "truly know."

Thus, at times when the Bible speaks of the heart, it is pointing to this dimension of deep-seated knowledge and understanding. This form of knowing particularly pertains to the believer whose heart has been regenerated and illuminated through the indwelling of the Holy Spirit. This is not some kind of esoteric knowledge reserved only for a spiritually elite, as the Gnostic heretics in the second through fourth centuries held to. It is an understanding that is at once experiential or personal and at the same time reflective of ultimate truth that we seek to discern through the mind. This kind of knowledge is possible because God's inner work creates receptivity to that knowledge. Biblically such knowledge is also closely tied to the notion of wisdom, which is an understanding that goes beyond facts and data to discernment in applying knowledge to the daily routines of life.

The Proverbs often link the heart to understanding or wisdom. For example, "the discerning heart seeks knowledge," and "the heart of the righteous weighs its answers" (15:14, 28 NIV). The book of Deuteronomy, called by some "the book of the heart," links the knowing and keeping of God's law with the heart, "for this will show your wisdom and discernment to the peoples" (4:6; compare Deut 6:4-6). The psalmists talk of speaking "the truth from their heart" (15:2), "meditation of my heart" (19:14; 49:3), and "the law of their God in their hearts" (37:31; compare 119). In Colossians 2:2-3 Paul speaks of the heart having "assured understanding" and "the knowledge of God's mystery, that is Christ himself, in whom are hidden all the treasures of wisdom and knowledge." Jesus links the heart to understanding when he says to his disciples, "Do you still not perceive or understand? Are your hearts hardened? Do you have eyes, and fail to see? Do you have ears, and fail to hear?" (Mk 8:17-18; see also Mt 13:13). Thus it seems clear that the heart not only predisposes us to accept certain intellectual paradigms or reflections of the head, but the heart itself contains deep-seated thoughts and understandings.

The heart then is a configuration of these four elements: will, affections, feelings and understanding. They are often so closely tied together that we cannot differentiate them, though at times, based on the context, the focus may be on one or two particular dimensions of the heart.

THE ROLE OF THE HEART

Saul began his role as king with humility, with trust in God and with the affirmations of the people of Israel. He had charisma, a sense of authority and great physical stature to accompany these assets. But the story of this great king in the Bible is the story of a downward spiral into fear, jealousy, hatred, spiritual rebellion and even the occult. What went wrong with this talented political leader?

The main problem for Saul was not his beliefs about God, but his heart's sensibility toward God and God's ways. As a result his actions began to reflect rebellion against God. When Samuel the prophet told Saul that his days as king were over, he added, "The LORD has sought out a man after his own heart; and the LORD has appointed him to be ruler over his people" (1 Sam 13:14).

The heart plays a crucial role in life and particularly in our spiritual journey. We can never hope to be whole or holy until our hearts are brought close to our Maker. But what specifically does the heart do in our Christian life? We will examine its role in conversion, spirituality, character and moral actions.

The heart in conversion. In chapter two we saw that true conversion to Christ involves the mind, because there is cognitive content to the gospel. But clearly a faith of the mind with cognitive assent to right beliefs is not true faith if it is not also accompanied by a commitment of the heart. After all, as James put it, "You believe that God is one; you do well.

Even the demons believe—and shudder" (2:19). The heart and the head must come together in saving faith, for "if you confess with your lips that Jesus is Lord and believe in your heart that God raised him from the dead, you will be saved. For one believes with the heart and so is justified, and one confesses with the mouth and so is saved" (Rom 10:9-10).

The role of the heart in conversion involves our will, our affections and our understanding. When one comes to Christ, there is an inner redirection, with change of allegiances and recognition of the true meaning of salvation. There is an inner assent and commitment that comes from the very core of the person's being, effected not by one's own natural capacities but through the supernatural work of the triune God. In conversion there is a redirection of our affections, so that we now come to love God in ways we never imagined.

The work of God in salvation in turn further impacts the heart, including the emotions. The new inward feelings that flow from divine regeneration are well captured by Edwards, as he reflects on his own conversion:

> The first instance that I remember of the sort of inward, sweet delight in God and divine things that I have lived much in since was on reading these words, 1 Timothy 1:17, "Now unto the King eternal, immortal, invisible, the only wise God, be honour and glory for ever and ever, Amen." As I read these words, there came into my soul, and was as it were diffused through it, a sense of the glory of the Divine Being; a new sense, quite different from anything I ever experienced before. Never any words of scripture seemed to me as these words did. I thought with myself, how excellent a Being that was, and how happy I should be, if I might enjoy that God.[11]

The great conversion stories of people like Augustine, Luther, Wesley and C. S. Lewis all reflect a similar impact on their feelings: peace, consolation, joy, surprise.

When people reject Christ as Savior and Lord, they do so out of far more than cognitive beliefs. The Bible often speaks of darkened hearts and hardened hearts (for example, Mk 3:5; Jn 12:40; Rom 2:5), which preclude people from taking the step of faith and commitment. A person whose will is bent on self-direction, whose affections are toward idols of this world and whose understandings lack insights into God's spiritual dealings with humanity will not generally be open to a salvation by God's grace through the death and resurrection of Christ, resulting in a transformation of life, lived for God's glory and the good of others.

I recall a conversation I once had with a young woman named Judy. She had been exposed to vital Christian faith through friends, but said, "I just never could bring myself to believe those kinds of things"— miracles, sin, grace, resurrection and the Trinity. As I probed a bit deeper with her, however, it was evident that her problem was not a cognitive rejection of the supernatural. Judy admitted that she read the horoscope daily, believed in reincarnation, thought that angels helped people out and believed there really was a life after death. She clearly had room for things beyond the natural realm. The real issue, as I discovered through further conversation, was that Judy's whole life centered on her own personal desires and self-centered ambitions. She truly believed that she had the goods within to resolve all her problems and struggles. It was a self-sufficient heart and pride that kept her from the kingdom of God— the same sentiments that sent our first human parents spiraling out of Eden and God's presence into a fallen state.

The heart in Christian growth (spirituality). Coming to Christ in faith is the beginning of a wonderful journey of growing not only in knowledge about God and his kingdom in the intellectual sense but also in knowledge of God and his kingdom in the personal, experiential sense. Many people today tend to equate spirituality with the heart, but merely giving attention to the inner self is not at all true, God-centered spirituality. In a sense, all people experience some kind of "spiritual" formation. As Willard wrote, "Terrorists as well as saints are the outcome of spiritual formation. Their spirits or hearts have been formed."[12] The question is, by what and to what are our hearts formed?

Christian growth and spirituality are particularly centered in the heart in terms of God's progressive work of transformation into the image of Christ. The head and the hands always work in conjunction with the heart in this process, but no growth occurs without a significant transformation of the heart. Our will, affections, feelings and understandings must constantly be under renovation if we are to develop Christlikeness, the goal of spiritual formation.

There is a tendency to sometimes equate the spiritual disciplines (prayer, meditation, fasting, giving, etc.) with spirituality. But they are merely the mechanisms for spiritual growth, not the essence of spirituality itself. As a matter of fact, Jesus hit rather hard on spiritual disciplines that had become unhinged from true spirituality of the heart. The Pharisees were examples par excellence of practicing the disciplines, but of them he said, "This people honors me with their lips, / but their hearts are far from me; / in vain do they worship me, / teaching human precepts as doctrines" (Mk 7:6-7).

If sin is the major barrier to spirituality, we must recognize the link between sin and our inward passions. In Mark 7 the Pharisees, with their spiritual zeal and disciplines, confronted Jesus and his disciples for eating with defiled hands, having not gone through the ceremonial washing of the religious tradition. Jesus responded that it is not the external things (such as food or germs) that go in and defile the person, but rather the things that come from within that truly defile (v. 15). After the crowds left and he was alone with his disciples, Jesus furthered their understanding:

> "Do you not see that whatever goes into a person from outside cannot defile, since it enters, not the heart but the stomach, and goes out into the sewer?" (Thus he declared all foods clean.) And he said, "It is what comes out of a person that defiles. For it is from within, from the human heart, that evil intentions come: fornication, theft, murder, adultery, avarice, wickedness, deceit, licentiousness, envy, slander, pride, folly. All these evil things come from within, and they defile a person." (vv. 18-23)

Spiritual formation never comes merely by a cognizance of human sin, but it is a starting point. Thus Jesus was attempting to refocus the pharisaical perception that external rites alone could do the job. Unless we can deal with the internal vices, we can never go on to righteous being and doing.

Spiritual formation and maturity come as the will, affections, feelings and understandings say yes to the promptings of the Holy Spirit to be led more and more in the direction of Christ's image and his kingdom. In this process the captivity of a sinful heart gives way to a heart freed in Christ to righteousness and to a life in which the fruit of the Spirit are evident. As Paul put it, "Thanks be to God that you, having once been slaves of sin, have become obedient from the heart to the form of teaching to which you were entrusted, and that you, having been set free from sin, have become slaves of righteousness" (Rom 6:17-18).

Part of spiritual development is allowing our inward selves to be overwhelmed by the love and presence of God in Christ. In his own journey, Manning discovered that his experience of God's unfathomable love was thwarted because of self-hatred and a self-imposed burden to right his own wrongs. It was only when he came to acknowledge this brokenness within his heart that he could then open himself up to God's healing within. Manning writes, "We learn to be gentle with ourselves by experiencing the intimate, heartfelt compassion of Jesus. To the extent that we allow the relentless tenderness of Jesus to invade the citadel of self, we are free from dyspepsia toward ourselves."[13]

The heart and personal character. Throughout much of the modern world, ethical thought focused on actions and the right thing to do. In recent years a number of philosophers and theologians have returned to an old tradition, harking back to the Greek philosopher Aristotle and to some thinkers in the Middle Ages. These folks argue that the core of ethical living is not what we do, but who we are—character. Character, they believe, is formed by virtues within, which are modeled and taught in specific communities with a given narrative, or moral framework. These writers lament modernity's moral fixation on laws, principles and the calculation of consequences.

While I don't personally buy all that the virtue ethicists contend for, they are certainly right to bring character and virtue back into the moral agenda. And they are right to remind us that true morality and good ethical actions usually flow from a virtuous heart. My primary disagreement is with their overemphasis on character to the exclusion of attending to action and their narrowing of our ethical resources to narratives, thus precluding the guidance of moral laws and principles.

What is character? The best definition I can think of came from my seventh-grade Sunday school teacher, who was the best teacher I ever had. He was memorable not so much for what he taught, for I recall more discussions about the Philadelphia Phillies (usually hapless and in last place in those days) than about the Bible or the Christian life. He was remarkable for who he was and the care he showed to a rowdy group of boys. But there was one thing I never forgot from that teacher. He said, "Character is who we are when nobody's looking." In other words, character is my heart, the real inner me.

Our character is the moral bent of our will, affections, feelings and understandings. And we will never develop moral character without a focus on these heart dimensions. Our compassion for others, our integrity, our sense of justice (racial, economic and so on), our commitment to human dignity, our sexual purity, our contentment with what we have and our love of rightness are a result of a heart that is formed toward the very character and actions of God himself. Morality is not primarily about universal principles and rules that merely exist in nature, though by natural reason and experience we may know something of true morality. Rather, morality is ultimately rooted in God's character and actions.

Therefore true moral character must always be a spiritual enterprise, arising from grace, sustained by the Spirit of the living God. Of course all humans can gain some sense of God's designs for life. This comes because of the way God has created the world and the image of God that still resides within all humans, albeit in fallen form. But the true moral character reflecting Christlikeness in all domains of daily existence comes from a heart that has been renovated by God's grace and the work of his Holy Spirit.

The heart and moral actions. It only follows that if God's work in the heart is a key to moral character, then the heart is also a key to moral actions. Of course such is never void of the mind, as we saw earlier, because it is with the mind that we know God's designs for moral action. Moreover, the mind also plays even a motivational role in what we do.

Jesus taught not only that our sinful actions arise from our heart, but that good moral actions do as well. One day, in the context of talking about hypocrisy with his disciples, Jesus said that "no good tree bears bad fruit, nor again does a bad tree bear good fruit" (Lk 6:43). Our Lord drew his lessons from nature as he reminded them that "each tree is known by its own fruit. Figs are not gathered from thorns, nor are grapes picked from a bramble bush" (Lk 6:44). What is true in nature is true in human life, for "the good person out of the good treasure of the heart produces good, and the evil person out of evil treasure produces evil; for it is out of the abundance of the heart that the mouth speaks" (Lk 6:45).

Thus the character ethicists are right to remind us that what we do is often a mirror of who we are. When we face moral choices in life, we almost intuitively do the right thing when our passions have been formed in the right direction. Both our personal ethic choices and our social ethic commitments are reflections of our heart. For example, acts of racism aren't just random acts. They reflect a heart of prejudice in which people find false security in their own physical or cultural identity, viewing others different from themselves as a threat. What starts in the human heart eventually finds its way into the cultural fabric and societal institutions. In one sense, racist laws and policies have a life of their own, in that they are no longer dependent on the heart and actions of particular people in specific situations. But ultimately they stem from fallen human hearts that need God's cleansing and renewing.

We face many difficult moral challenges today in business, government, law, education, medicine, science, church and social services. Many of the issues that confront us are complex, and the choices of the good, right and just are not immediately evident. Our moral character will not give us an immediate answer on the tough questions, but it does provide the context in which we will need to use our minds to understand the nature of the issues and the best course of action. And, without hearts that are sensitive to God's designs, human need and the common good, we will never be able to choose the good in those complex situations that face us, no matter how deep and profound our thinking may be. Being passionate about the ethically good is a prerequisite for doing it.

This is particularly true when we recognize that many of our moral choices and actions will at times fly in the face of the status quo, the cultural norms. Only inner selves that are formed toward Christ and empowered by God's Spirit from within will have the resolve to go against the grain and endure the social pressures of the crowd. If we do not have a Christ-centered heart, the sentiments of our world will dislodge us from God's deepest intentions for our lives—intentions that are true, good and beautiful.

DISCUSSION QUESTIONS

1. In your own words describe the four dimensions of the heart described in this chapter. What are some of the ways you have experienced the heart as will, affections, emotions and understanding?

2. What role did the heart play in your own conversion experience? How did the heart interact with head and hands in your conversion experience? How might we appeal to the heart in sharing Christ with nonbelievers?

3. What role does the heart play in your spirituality? How does the heart interact with head and hands in your own spiritual journey?

4. This chapter contends that the heart is important for both personal character and moral actions. Can you think of other biblical passages that support these roles of the heart? In your experience how important is the heart for character and moral action? How do you think we should appeal to the heart in relation to social and ethical issues in the larger culture?

5

DISTORTIONS OF THE HEART

In the opening chapter we met Jennifer, the social activist. Jennifer was deeply committed to putting her faith into practice in the trenches of a real and hurting world. She believed that a faith without acts of mercy and justice was no faith at all and a contradiction to everything Jesus stood for. Her commitments and involvements in racial, economic and environmental justice were laudatory, but the heart was missing. Jennifer's activism was not sustained by God-empowered inner affections and sentiments. A personal relationship with Christ had become a cause; faith had become social ethics. She reflected a "heartless" Christianity, a distortion of biblical faith.

But we also encountered Christina, who made the opposite mistake. Her entire life was directed by the heart and particularly by the feelings of the heart. The mind and actions were of little significance for the way she lived her life, for the inner power and presence of God were all that mattered. Christina had a faith expression ruled by passion, another form of heart distortion.

Both Jennifer and Christina exhibited distortions of the heart—the one from neglect, the other from overemphasis. In this chapter we explore what happens when these distortions appear, and ways to nurture the heart to prevent them from occurring.

WHEN THE HEART IS NEGLECTED

Christ calls us to love God with heart, soul and mind (Mt 22:37). But what happens when the heart is missing or minimized? What impacts can we discern for life in general as well as for our faith? We find that the results are profound. As John Wesley once put it in a sermon:

> A man may be orthodox in every point; he may not only espouse right opinions, but zealously defend them against all opposers; he may think justly concerning the incarnation of our Lord, concerning the ever blessed Trinity, and every other doctrine contained in the oracles of God. . . . He may be almost as orthodox as the devil . . . and may all the while be as great a stranger as he to the religion of the heart.[1]

Loss of divine presence and power. All human beings seem to have a quest for presence and power. Men and women long to have a personal touch whereby they feel the nearness and care not just of others, but of an Other. We hunger for the personal presence of transcendence in our lives in order to know that in this great cosmos we matter and are cared for. Humans also long for personal power. In our moments of fragility, ineptitude and failure, we hunger for a power beyond ourselves to enable us to transcend our foibles and sins. Presence and power seem to be universal needs of the human race.

In biblical faith the Holy Spirit in particular grants presence and power to those who have said yes to God's grace. The Father and the Son are, of course, part of these wonderful gifts, for we can never separate too far the persons of the one God. But in the Bible it is particularly the Holy Spirit who is present in our moments of perceived abandon and who grants power in our times of helplessness. In Romans 8 Paul reminds us that anyone who belongs to Christ has the Holy Spirit living within them. Therefore, he wrote, "If the Spirit of him who raised Jesus from the dead dwells in you, he who raised Christ from the dead will give life to your mortal bodies also through his Spirit that dwells in you" (v. 11).

The presence and power of the Spirit are primarily within, that is, in our hearts. Therefore, if we have a heartless faith, our experience of these gifts of grace will be limited. It is in the heart that we begin to experience what many writers of spirituality term intimacy with God, or even a vision of God. Without attention to the heart, God will essentially be an idea, a force or a principle. This is always the danger of neglecting the inner side of faith: God becomes impersonal. Thus the personal touch of God in our lives is missing: comfort, joy, peace, consolation, feeling forgiven, boldness to face the unknown and empowerment for difficult tasks.

If we don't nurture the heart, we can never grow into deeper relationship with God. In fact the personal relationship dimension will be thwarted, and spiritual vitality will be lacking. Spirituality will essentially become a set of beliefs and a course of actions. True spirituality, on the other hand, will open one's will, affections, feelings and inner thoughts to the personal touch of the Spirit and the power of God to transform us. As Jonathan Edwards pointed out, true religion consists of holy affections, which always bring with them a sense of spiritual vitality and aliveness. A heartless faith will appear bleak and tepid. Friendship with God will be missing, as will divine consolation and strength for life's most difficult challenges.

Only with the heart will we truly know God in the biblical sense of knowing. Only then can we sing with the psalmist, "How lovely is your dwelling place, / O LORD of Hosts! My soul longs, indeed it faints / for the courts of the LORD; / my heart and my flesh sing for joy / to the living God" (84:1-2).

In opening our hearts to God's work we then discover the heart of God personally. As Richard Foster wrote, "Today the heart of God is an open wound of love. He aches over our distance and preoccupation. He

mourns that we do not draw near to him. . . . He weeps over our obses-
sion with muchness and manyness. He longs for our presence."[2]

Loss of mystery. When Christian faith is limited to the head or the
hands and the heart's significance is minimized, believers find it difficult
to come to terms with the sense of mystery that we encounter in both
Christian thought and Christian experience. Head faith tends to focus on
rationality, logic and ideas; it has great difficulty dealing with any sense
of mystery, ambiguity, the unknown, wonder, awe or transcendence insofar as it touches one personally. Hands faith tends to focus so much on
actions that it fails to adequately deal with anything that isn't concrete or
clear in its outcomes. Only when the head and hands are joined with the
heart can we come to terms with those parts of reality and faith that we
can't fully grasp or contain.

There are mysteries in following Christ. The word *mystery* appears
thirty times in the New Testament, as it speaks of the mystery of the
kingdom, of Christ, of the gospel, of the faith and of the resurrection of
the body (for example, Mk 4:11; Rom 11:25; 16:25; 1 Cor 15:51; Eph
1:9; 3:3-6). *Mystery* refers to those elements of Christian thought and life
that are hidden in the sense that they are not routinely understood by
human experience or reason. At times *mystery* implies a reality so foreign
to our natural senses that we recognize we will never fully grasp or understand it.

We encounter mystery in theology with doctrines such as that of the
Trinity. We never can fully grasp how God can be one and three. We encounter mystery, or at least I believe that we should, when we reflect on
how God's sovereignty and human freedom can fit together. The mystery
of this divine reality escapes our finite ruminations, as we recognize that
"as the heavens are higher than the earth, / so are my ways higher than
your ways / and my thoughts than your thoughts" (Is 55:9).

We also come across mystery in the ebb and flow of life, especially the
challenging experiences. When we undergo what we perceive to be un-
deserved suffering or pain, or excruciating loss of something dear to us

(that is, a spouse, child, friend, job, marriage), we want to know what God is up to. In those moments we often experience what we think to be the silence of God and can only respond to the mystery with a sense of wonder and awe.

Recognizing mystery in the things we cannot understand is integral to our spiritual journey. If we could figure it all out we'd never need to trust, pray and wait. Vital spirituality needs a sense of mystery to grow deeper in Christ. It is not just through explicit knowledge of the nature and ways of God that we learn to trust and abandon ourselves into the hands of a merciful Savior. It is rather in mystery that we cast ourselves on a God far beyond us, yet always here with us.

Mystery is also essential for deep and true worship of the triune God. Liturgies, music and prayers that exude a cognitive certainty that appears to have God figured out do little to generate awe and wonder in the face of our Creator. It is in experiencing some mystery surrounding God's nature and ways that we are prone to a worship of awe, majesty and silence. And it is primarily through the heart that we sense the splendor of a God who cannot be fully grasped in the finitude of our mind. Without the heart we fail to be silent before God. Without passion we fail to cry out in the uncertainties and ambiguities of mystery, "I believe, help my unbelief" (Mk 9:24). Only in allowing for mystery is profound worship and living trust truly possible. And only with attentiveness to the heart do we encounter such mystery.

Loss of character—replaced with legalism. We have already discussed the biblical role of the heart in developing moral character. It only follows that when the heart is neglected, moral character is lacking. And when moral character is lacking, there is a tendency to turn to legalism to shore up one's moral life. Legalism not only focuses on moral laws for laws' sake, but also tends to add human-made rules to the moral arena.

This was precisely the problem Jesus had with the Pharisees of his day. They gave scrupulous attention to the details of the law and developed human interpretations of the law, which eventually became as

authoritative as the law itself. Thus, in pronouncing woe on the Pharisees and Scribes because of their hypocrisy, Jesus said, "You tithe mint,
dill, and cumin, and have neglected the weightier matters of the law: justice and mercy and faith. It is these you ought to have practiced without
neglecting the others. You blind guides! You strain out a gnat but swal-
low a camel!" (Mt 23:23-24).

They had lost all sense of perspective on the law of God, because they
failed to develop a heart for God. Thus Jesus said to them, "You clean the
outside of the cup and of the plate, but inside they are full of greed and
self-indulgence. You blind Pharisee! First clean the inside of the cup, so
that the outside also may become clean" (Mt 23:25-26). The root problem for these religious leaders was that they had given such attention to
enunciating the details of the law (head) and keeping the law outwardly
(hands), that they had failed to nurture the inward, passionate side of
life. Quoting the prophet Isaiah, Jesus said of them, "This people honors
me with their lips, / but their hearts are far from me; / in vain do they
worship me, / teaching human precepts as doctrines" (Mk 7:6-7).

Such is generally the plight of those who neglect the heart. I recall the
father of Jill, an acquaintance of mine. He was a legalist to the core. What
Jill heard in her dad's faith as she was growing up was a rigid set of reg-
ulations: no movies, no dancing, no earrings, no sports on Sundays, no
Bible other than the King James Version and no friendship with "pagans." Her father seemed to show no inward love for Christ, only an ad-
herence to a set of beliefs and a code of rules. Affection and emotion were
missing in relating to God and to his daughter. Parenthood was about
enforcing rules and so was Christianity. Sad to say, today Jill no longer
calls herself a believer. When the heart is missing, moral character gives
way to legalism, an enemy of vital Christian faith.

Loss of true understanding. As noted earlier, it may come as a surprise to learn that our understanding of the faith is impacted by inatten-
tion to the heart. But a significant dimension of the heart consists of
deep-seated thoughts and understanding. Thus, as one theologian has

noted, theology is "an inquiry which requires personal involvement and an inspiration to know and love God." Furthermore, "there is no detached knowing of God any more than there is a detached love of neighbor or a detached attitude toward one's failure to obey God."[3]

In the Christian faith there is an objective side that certainly transcends our human perceptions and responses. Our subjective spiritual experiences should always be rooted in the reality of God and divine revelation. As David Naugle put it, "Worldview in Christian perspective implies the objective existence of the Trinitarian God whose essential character establishes the moral order of the universe and whose word, wisdom and law define and govern all aspects of created existence."[4] However, as we seek to understand in human categories the nature and work of the triune God, as revealed in Scripture and understood through the ages, we do so not merely through the head, but also through the heart. Our will, affections and emotions all play a role in what we perceive about the objective side of our faith.

Of course there are potential pitfalls in this process, but when the heart is attuned to God, we come to understand our faith in deeper and more profound ways. Moreover, when our heart is not attuned to God, we can be sure that it will negatively impact our understanding of God and his ways (theology) and of God's designs for daily living (ethics).

The sentiments of our heart are not the source of our theology and ethics in terms of content, but the state of our heart is the precondition for our theology and ethics. The heart forms the basic orientation of our lives, and through that orientation we come to understand, believe and affirm. Augustine, John Calvin, Jonathan Edwards, John Wesley, Ellen Charry and a host of other theologians and leaders in the church have reminded us that our understandings of God and the essentials of our faith are deeply intertwined with the condition of our heart. Thus theology and spirituality can never be separated.

I have observed on various occasions people who have experienced a "crisis of faith" or have even "lost their faith." For some it has even oc-

curred in the midst of studying theology and the Bible. In every case I
can think of, it was not merely a crisis of intellectual beliefs. It seemed
to always include issues of the heart.

I think of one acquaintance in my graduate studies. Steve came into
graduate work in theology with a deep commitment to understanding the
faith in order to enable the church to find its way amid the competing
claims of a pluralistic culture. But he failed to give attention to his inner
spiritual life. Gradually he came to spend little time in personal devotions
and worship of God and only read the Bible when it pertained to his intellectual pursuits. He had gone through a difficult experience in ministry
and was bitter in the aftermath. The bitterness ate at the very fabric of his
soul. Even his wife felt that affections toward her were distant and hard.
When Steve eventually declared that he no longer believed in the deity of
Christ, the authority of the Bible and the necessity of personal redemption in Christ, it was a reflection of an embittered, distant heart.

Our will, affections, patterns of emotions and deep-seated understandings have a powerful impact on what we believe and follow in life.
Though the head is important for our spiritual journey, it can never lead
us well without a heart that is sensitive to God and in turn sensitive to
our neighbors and to the true condition of ourselves. And as Roman
Catholic theologian Mary Jo Weaver has so aptly put it, "When the heart
is rooted in God, the mind is free to play. Free to have fun."[5] The human
mind, liberated by a godly heart, never exists in a vacuum. Its "playful"
liberation is rooted in God, mediated through the truth of the gospel and
the truth of God's Word, for as Jesus said, "You will know the truth, and
the truth will make you free" (Jn 8:32).

WHEN PASSION RULES

Though the heart is essential to a whole faith for the whole person, it can
never operate alone or apart from thought and action. As we saw in the
first chapter, throughout the history of the Christian church some believers have seen the heart as the exclusive source and guide for faith. There

is much to learn from their imbalances and mistakes. A faith focused exclusively or primarily on passion is destined to lead us down blind alleys for life in general and for our faith in particular.

Vulnerable to inward states. Even though the heart may be the locus of good things through the work of God, an excessive internal focus is vulnerable to abuses. When we attend only to the heart, it is easy to allow our internal state to define our faith. At times our experiences or even our physical condition can influence the sentiments of our heart, and when we focus primarily on the heart, those experiences and conditions make us especially vulnerable spiritually.

All of us go through times when our inward self is not consistent with the affirmations of our mind. Our emotions take over, and we come to doubt what our head tells us. Our affections turn cold, and we feel that God must not care. Our will gets distorted in its aims, and the passions of our heart appear wayward. No matter how spiritually mature we are, our inward self at times goes through these experiences. If our faith is focused primarily on the heart, we will be susceptible to these inner impulses when they occur. God will be there when we feel joy or peace, but will be deemed absent when we fill sadness and inner turmoil.

When I was in the pastorate, there were occasional times when I did not feel emotionally or spiritually up to preaching. Fortunately I quickly learned that preaching was not primarily about my emotional states, but about God's Word. Though my inward self was deeply involved in preaching, the act of preaching and the object of my preaching were not ultimately about me, but about Christ and his Word. Thankfully the truth and reality of God transcend our "innards," and I always took consolation in that fact in my low moments.

This in no way means we should overlook the subjective feelings we may experience at a given point in time. I have also learned that they may be symptomatic of very real issues that we need to confront. But there are also times when the state of our inward self must not dictate our spirituality and the basic course of our life.

Our vulnerability to emotional and affectional states is real because of their intimate relationship with bodily states. At various times in life's journey, the very nature of our physiological processes impacts our inward sentiments. Physical pain, physiologically induced depression, illness or physical changes associated with the human life cycle are cases in point. Thus the heart is challenged by what we feel in our bodies.

At other times our inward state is affected by circumstances around us or by our relationships with others. If our faith in Christ is primarily heart-oriented, we will be especially vulnerable to these changing inward states.

Ricardo was a college student who came to see me one day, convinced that Christ and the Bible no longer made sense. He had become doubtful that God could make any difference in his life. As we talked, it became evident that Ricardo had frequently experienced these sentiments, only to then jubilantly rebound with very fervent faith. Up and down his spiritual mood went ricocheting from one extreme to another. As we talked, it became clear that Ricardo's faith was built on what he felt, so that Jesus was "real" only when he was personally feeling good, and the Bible was "true" only when he got positive inward vibes from reading it. Fortunately, through spiritual mentoring, Ricardo came to realize that the reality of genuine faith was not dependent on his feelings. His growth with God began to flourish.

Ricardo came to understand that if we allow passion to rule, we will be vulnerable to our inward states. God will be real when we *feel* him to be real. But God will be absent or uncaring when we don't *feel* him to be real. We all at times have such feelings. But our faith is particularly vulnerable to those feelings when we focus exclusively or primarily on the heart in our spiritual development.

Inadequate resources for engaging the world. Historically one of the dangers of a faith of the heart is the failure to engage the world. By its very nature this inward-focused type of faith finds it difficult to move outward in cultural engagement for the glory of God. While adherents of mysticism and Pentecostalism have sometimes given lip service to interacting with the world as salt and light, their very inward orientation tends to limit such interaction. It is no accident that many of the mystics of the Middle Ages were also monastics who had committed themselves to a life apart from society and culture.

But beyond the natural proclivity away from the world, a faith of the heart also often lacks necessary resources for cultural engagement. A heart attuned to God's purposes and leading certainly has the motivation for cultural engagement, if it is on the radar screen. Indeed, without the heart, the motivation and power for such engagement will be missing. But a faith of the heart alone will not provide the understandings essential for a journey within the world, with its vexing challenges. A faith with heartfelt zeal but no light will soon be led astray; light and heat by nature go together.

To engage the world in both evangelism and social concern we need a clear understanding of the world. Adherents to a faith of the heart have sometimes done a good job with evangelism. But their evangelism has frequently been otherworldly, lacking the needed cognitive understanding of how faith in Christ makes a concrete difference in the world. Such evangelism has also tended to lack contextualization, the attempt to express the gospel and a Christian worldview with language and methods appropriate for the setting. A faith of the heart often nourishes a zeal for sharing the faith, but lacks wisdom in methods for evangelism and strategies for in-depth discipleship. Thus this approach has at times produced large numbers of converts, but converts who frequently are not discipled in a way that enables them to face the world and the challenges of everyday life.

Such shallowness certainly carries over to cultural engagement, in which believers seek to be salt and light. A faith in which passion rules simply does not have the necessary theological and cultural understandings for such engagement. As a result the world may be abandoned in favor of an inward faith away from its challenges and temptations. Iron-

ically such an approach to culture can be most vulnerable to the pernicious side of culture.

Heterodoxy. Just as an excessive faith of the head can lead to heterodox theology, so too can an excessive faith of the heart. Heterodox formulations abandon biblical and theological understandings, articulated
and tested by the Christian church over the long haul, in favor of more
immediate sentiments of the heart. While the heart is necessary for true
biblical and theological understanding, banking on the heart alone will
most likely lead us astray.

One of the clearest examples of this can be seen in the potential danger to turn mysticism into pantheism. A good example of this was Meis-
ter Eckhart, the fourteenth-century German mystic. He so emphasized
the absorption of the self with God in a mystical experience that there
was no longer a clear distinction between God and the person. More recent examples reflect how one can fall prey to a type of pantheism by
making the soul divine and the actual source of spirituality, rather than
the locus of spirituality. In the mid-twentieth century a Quaker philosopher wrote, "Deep within us all there is an amazing inner sanctuary of
the soul, a holy place, a Divine Center, a speaking Voice, to which we
may continuously return. Eternity is at our hearts, pressing on our time-
torn lives, warming us with intimations of an astounding destiny, calling
us home unto Itself."[6]

This quote is sometimes used in contemporary discussions of spirituality to emphasize the need for silence and listening to God. But there
are several dangers in this statement as it stands. First, the soul itself is
seen as the source of our spiritual vitality; second, capitalization of certain words seem to imply that the soul has a divine nature. Our inner
self, whether defined as the soul or the heart, is not divine and of itself
is not the ultimate source of spirituality. God, who is distinct from us, is
the source of our spirituality and does his work deep within our hearts.
To esteem the soul as divine or to make it the ultimate source of spirituality seems to come close to a form of pantheism in which the divine-

human distinction is blurred. In this approach, divine resources for life lie within ourselves, rather than with the Creator of the universe, who comes to reside within us.

People today are "into spirituality." In surveys of religious beliefs and practices in Western societies, many people say that they are not religious but are deeply spiritual.[7] Contemporary forms of spirituality tend toward a very individualized, inner search that leads people away from classical formulations that are rooted in Scripture. Thus contemporary spiritual quests are frequently preoccupied with reincarnation, the presence of personal angels, the preexistence of the soul and the primacy of self-actualization to discover one's inner self. Such forms of spirituality are neither rooted in the triune God of the universe nor guided by the Bible. Usually these internal spiritual quests are not accountable to a body of believers. Thus unorthodox versions of "spiritual faith" abound with a primacy of the heart, apart from the head and the hands.

One of the most obvious abuses in excesses of the heart is when emotions are allowed to dictate beliefs and experiences. A clear danger of this can be seen historically in some of the excesses that occasionally accompanied revivalism. Revivals, or awakenings, have played a significant role in revitalizing the church when they have been guided by solid theological reflection, accompanied by fruits of love, mercy, justice and witness to the larger world. Such was the case for the most part in the First Awakening, with the leadership of people like Jonathan Edwards. In this Awakening the revival was not conjured up by manipulation of people's emotions and was usually not even expected by those awakened.

But revivalism has not always brought true revitalization and spiritual depth. In fact sometimes it has lead to schism, conflict, confusion and heterodox theology and morals. For example, the "burned-over district" of western New York experienced wave after wave of revivalism in the early nineteenth century. But the people of the area were so focused on experiential and emotional religiosity that these communities also became the breeding ground for numerous sects and cults. Mormonism, spiritualism, Shakerism, extreme forms of perfectionism and the Oneida Community with its sexual communitarianism all emerged and flourished in this area.[8] Revivalism, when focused primarily on emotional experience without the guidance of the Bible, theology and the wisdom of the larger church, has the potential to be heart religion run amuck.

NURTURING THE HEART

Though we cannot live by heart alone, we cannot live without it either. But what nurtures and sustains the heart? What do we need for the heart to play a vital and balanced role in our Christian experience—one that can avoid the distortions?

Spiritual disciplines. There are, of course, varied listings of the spiritual disciplines, but among the primary disciplines listed are prayer, silence, meditation on God's Word, fasting, service and reflection. These are a key element in shaping the contours of our heart. As noted earlier, the disciplines are not themselves spirituality, but rather are exercises that can enable our inner selves to grow in Christlikeness and deep friendship with the triune God. The disciplines are precisely that: disciplined exercises that enable our thinking, inner sentiments and actions to reflect godliness and righteousness in all areas of life. The disciplines particularly help us to more clearly see and hear God and to discern God's purposes for humanity and our personal lives.

The spiritual disciplines impact our thinking and our actions, but are most significant for forming Christlikeness in the depth of our being. Richard Foster has pointed out that in an age of superficiality, instant gratification is a major spiritual problem. He writes, "The desperate need today is not for a greater number of intelligent . . . or gifted people, but for deep people. The classical disciplines of the spiritual life call us to move beyond surface living into the depths."[9] They are called disciplines because they require personal discipline, which then becomes habitual and hence shapes both the inner and outer dimensions of life.

Worship. Individual and corporate worship is also important for nurturing the inner life. True worship comes from the heart, and thus a vital encounter with God in specific acts of worship enables our inner selves to go deeper and to be sensitized to spiritual realities. We do not engage in worship primarily for the benefits we receive, for then it can become consumerist and superficial. We worship the triune God of the universe because it is a fitting response to who God is. But one of the byproducts of other-centered worship (as opposed to self-centered) is that it nurtures and shapes our will, affections, feelings and understanding in the direction of Christ's kingdom.

In the contemporary wars over worship, we are frequently focused on styles or modes of worship. The debates lose sight of the true nature of worship and its potential for nurturing our hearts, individually and collectively, toward God. The forms and styles are important insofar as they are means of contextualizing worship appropriate to cultural and personality characteristics. But a fixation on the forms will lose sight of the ability of worship to bring us closer to God and to sensitize our hearts to the things of God. True and vital worship of God actually nurtures the inner dimension of our selves. By its nature, worship moves us away from mere thought and action into the deepest recesses of our being— the heart.

Attention to the aesthetic side of life. Sensitizing the heart to spirituality and deepening our inward relationship to God can also be aided by giving attention to the aesthetic side of life, an engagement with and appreciation of beauty. In pragmatic, result-oriented cultures we often see aesthetics as superfluous and certainly not related to spirituality. But in the Bible we are frequently drawn to the beauty of nature, God, worship and our final worship in heaven. Aesthetics, especially in contrast to our quest for results and success, has a powerful way of sensitizing us to the simple and natural things of life and a way of refreshing our inward selves. Allowing creativity to flourish and seeking aesthetic sensitivity draw us into a sphere of life and spirituality that a purely rational approach cannot achieve.

Appreciation of beauty (whether it be in nature, art or music) in and of itself is not spirituality. It does, however, create sensitivity in our hearts that can allow spirituality to flourish. Moreover, when we are attentive to aesthetics from the standpoint of God as the source of all beauty, our hearts are drawn to our Creator. Then we can recognize with the psalmist that "the heavens are telling the glory of God; / and the firmament proclaims his handiwork" (19:1).

Nurturing the heart for faithfulness to Christ is not merely giving attention to our inward selves. Such can be the height of self-centeredness and spiritual aberration. Nurturing the heart is preparing it for God to do a work of grace and renovation within. And even the preparation itself is ultimately from the hand of God.

DISCUSSION QUESTIONS

1. What has your experience been with heartless Christianity? Have you seen similar results as those described in this chapter? What other impacts have you seen when the heart is minimized?

2. This chapter talks about the loss of mystery when the heart is neglected. What role does mystery play in your own spiritual journey? What role do you believe it should play? Why is mystery hard for some Christians to accept?

3. What has your experience been with an expression of faith in which the heart rules? Have you observed similar results to those described in this chapter? What other impacts have you observed?

4. What role do the spiritual disciplines play in your walk with Christ? Do you believe the spiritual disciplines are overemphasized today? Underemphasized? What suggestions (other than the three mentioned at the end of this chapter) do you have for nurturing the heart?

6

CHRISTIAN FAITH
AND THE HANDS

Faith without works is dead. This is the verdict of the epistle of James (2:17) on a faith that is not tangibly demonstrated in real life. A person may have great biblical and theological understanding (the head) and exude with spiritual affections and feelings (the heart), but if one fails to express that faith in everyday living (the hands), it is empty and not genuine faith. Authentic Christianity is demonstrated through the most visible part of ourselves—the body. It is demonstrated by what we say and by what we do. Without such expression, our faith in Christ is vulnerable to perhaps the most frequent charge against Christians—the charge of hypocrisy.

Ryan and Susan both grew up in Christian homes. Their parents were involved in ministry; church, family devotions, Christian books and religious language permeated their socialization. They met in college and were drawn together by a common thread—a reaction to parents that "talked the talk" but failed to "walk the walk." Ryan and Susan felt that too often they had observed in their parents a strong belief without consistent actions. They saw strong religious emotion at church services and conferences, but at home there were emotional outbursts of anger and sarcasm. They saw their fathers, both pastors, speak frequently of God's love for the human race, but they felt little of that love personally.

Ryan and Susan began to share together their family woes; it became the bond of their relationship. Though they were in a Christian college, they began to question the validity of the Christian faith. They stopped going to church and chapel, no longer read their Bibles or prayed and, by the end of their sophomore year, declared that they wanted nothing to do with Christianity. They had seen a faith of the head and the heart, but the hands were missing. In their estimation such a faith was not worth the bother.

It is quite common to believe that if one has attended to the mind and the affections then Christian actions will be sure to follow. But it is not quite that simple. Just as some people may accentuate the head without the heart, so there are people who accentuate the head, the heart or both, without the hands. Unless our bodies and our actions, along with our minds and inner selves, are brought under the lordship of Christ, we will be incomplete believers. Faith without the hands is dead.

But what exactly are the hands? What kinds of action does the Bible call for? These are the questions I probe in this chapter.

EMBODIED FAITH

A faith of the hands is an embodied faith, demonstrated through the various parts of our body. We cannot understand the role of actions in faith without a biblical understanding of the physical body, for it plays a vital role, both positively and negatively.

The role of the body in Christianity. Some theologians have contended that Christianity is the most physical or material religion in the world. By this they are referring not to a love of money or a fixation on material things. Rather, in contrast to many religions and philosophies that find the body and material reality to be problematic, biblical faith strongly affirms things material, including the human body. Christian spirituality is not a freedom from the body, but a freedom within the body. Spiritual maturity comes not by negating our bodily dimension, but by harnessing its capacities and impulses for the glory of God through the work of God.

The significance of the body and material reality is grounded in several biblical and theological commitments. First, a theology of creation incorporates a strong affirmation of the material world with God's pronouncement of its goodness (Gen 1). Genesis 2:9 notes that "out of the ground the LORD God made to grow every tree that is pleasant to the sight and good for food." When God created humans in his image, "male and female he created them" (Gen 1:27), clearly implying that the biological and physiological side of life is significant.

Second, the body is affirmed in the incarnation: God taking on human flesh in his Son, Jesus Christ. That "the Word became flesh and lived among" (Jn 1:14) is a clear sign that the body in and of itself is not evil. If God can come in a human body, it is evidence that the body is not our primary foe spiritually. Rather, the incarnation is a model for our own lives.

Third, the physiological side of life is avowed through the future resurrection of the body. In our final abode we will not exist as disembodied souls, but as renewed or resurrected bodies. Such a notion would be foreign to a worldview in which the body is intrinsically evil or the primary barrier to goodness.

Of course our body, like our mind and our heart, bears the marks of the Fall, and as such is prone to lead us to sin. But God has created us to be in bodies. We might say that we are embodied souls, or ensouled bodies. Our bodies in and of themselves are not evil. They are a significant part of who we are and even have a role in influencing our thinking and the affections and emotions of our hearts. As Dallas Willard puts it, "My body is the original and primary place of my dominion and my responsibility. It is only through it that I have a world in which to live. That is why it, and not other physical objects in my world, is part of who I am and is essential to my identity. My life experiences come to me through or in conjunction with my body."[1]

Whenever we act within the world, we do so in our bodies. Our actions are certainly influenced by what we think, what we will, our emotional states, our affections and our contextual situation (that is, the world around us). But we can never act apart from our body. Our interaction with other people and the world in which God has placed us is always in and through it.

The body and sin. Though the body is not inherently evil, it is fallen and thus is often the locus and impetus for unrighteousness, injustice and moral failure. In Romans 6, in the context of clarifying freedom in Christ, Paul wrote, "Do not let sin exercise dominion in your mortal bodies, to make you obey their passions. No longer present your members to sin as instruments of wickedness, but present yourselves to God as those who have been brought from death to life, and present your members to God as instruments of righteousness" (vv. 12-13). Sin often reflects itself in bodily actions and within various parts of the human body, what Paul calls our members. These bodily actions reflect our thinking as well as our passions, but the body also has its own impulses and tendencies.

For example, James spoke of the deadly role of the tongue:

> The tongue is a small member, yet it boasts of great exploits. How great a forest is set ablaze by a small fire! And the tongue is a fire. The tongue is placed among our members as a world of iniquity; it stains the whole body, sets on fire the cycle of nature, and is itself set on fire by hell. . . . No one can tame the tongue—a restless evil, full of deadly poison. (3:5-6, 8)

The tongue, as James pointed out, has great potential for good, such as worshiping God and encouraging other people. But in its fallen state, this good gift of God also has a propensity for great damage and evil.

We can further understand the role of the body in sin when we think about sexual immorality. God has created our bodies good, and that includes our sexual parts as well. Yet, in our fallen state, the sexual parts can be misused. In 1 Corinthians 6 Paul reminds us that our "body is meant not for fornication but for the Lord" (v. 13). The body meant for the Lord includes the sexual dimension when it is utilized for God's glory, within the purposes and designs of God in creation. Even bodily pleasure in sex can be for the glory of God, for the physical parts that bring pleasure are gifts of God's good creation. But sexual immorality is a misuse of the bodily gift, forgetting "that [our] bodies are members of Christ" (v. 15). Thus, in sexual immorality (sexual intimacy outside God's designs), "the fornicator sins against the body itself" (v. 18).

We live in a time when the right to control our own body is deemed to be an absolute right. The judicial system in the United States (and in many other countries)[2] has extended bodily control to the right to snuff out another human life growing in one's own body. In a few countries and jurisdictions the right over one's body has been extended to ending one's own life when faced with extreme pain or physical debilitations. Euthanasia—or its narrower version, physician-assisted suicide—is really an extension of the ethos that we have an absolute right over our own body.

These kinds of sentiments are certainly understandable within a naturalistic worldview in which the body and material reality are the only givens. But solid reasoning, observation and historic experience can help us see the dead-end street to which this can lead. We are never isolated beings, and thus what we do with our bodies always impacts others and society. And Paul wrote, "Do you not know that your body is a temple of the Holy Spirit within you, which you have from God, and that you are not your own? For you were bought with a price; therefore glorify God in your body" (1 Cor 6:19-20).

The body and acts of goodness. Though our fallen bodies have a propensity for sin and injustice, the believer is called to use her body for good. Our hands, face, eyes, feet, stomach and genitals can be the instruments of evil but also instruments of righteousness, love and justice. The tongue that through slander, lies and cursing can cause so much pain to another person is the same tongue that can bring comfort and encouragement to another and adoration to God. The bodily parts that fornicate and even rape are the same parts that can express love to a spouse and generate the beginning of new human life. The key is that our bodies need to be brought under the lordship of Christ and the power of the Holy Spirit.

Just as the head and heart must experience the ongoing work of God's grace and transformation, so too must the body. Thus Paul wrote, "I appeal to you therefore, brothers and sisters, by the mercies of God, to present your bodies as a living sacrifice, holy and acceptable to God, which is your spiritual worship" (Rom 12:1). Here the focus is on commitment of our bodies as acts of worship to God through what we do in them. Not only are we to refrain from letting our bodies be under the domain of sin, but we are to "present [our] members to God as instruments of righteousness" (Rom 6:13).

This means that God's work within us will be demonstrated not only by what we refrain from doing, but also, and perhaps more significantly, by what we do. Our actions in everyday life are the real test of our faith and commitment to Christ. In one sense they are the natural overflow of a head and heart shaped by the work of God. Certainly bodily actions will never develop without a transformation of these dimensions. But we must also give attention to the body in the process. The body too must be made holy (that is, sanctified, in traditional language) so that we act for the glory of God.

CHRISTIAN ACTION: WORD AND DEED (PROCLAMATION AND PRESENCE)

Christians have sometimes been divided by their understanding of what God calls them to do. The church's perception of its mission to the world and of the responsibility of individuals in that mission have often created two competing camps: those who emphasize proclamation of the gospel, or evangelism, and those who emphasize acts of mercy, justice and service. The one side says that because the gospel is central in biblical faith, our primary calling in the world is to share the good news and invite people to experience reconciliation with God through Jesus Christ. The other side says that because love of neighbor is the command of Christ and because our bodies and emotions are integral to our identity, we must first address the temporal needs and social realities.

The divide between proponents of proclamation and presence, or word and deed, has often been quite wide. Sometimes it reflects real theological differences, as when the presence side has in the past denigrated or even changed the meaning of the gospel. Thus, in one version, "the aim of mission today is the humanization of society, by way of service to mankind." In this perspective "the demand is for tractors, not tracts," for "salvation has to do with personal and social liberation from everything that hinders man from attaining a true existence in justice and community."[3] Here proclamation is limited by a reinterpretation of the gospel.

Recently I heard a national radio interview with a clergyman who ran a "faith-based" ministry to gang members in the heart of a large city in America. This minister was adamant that it would be "cheap and inappropriate" for him to ever preach to these gangsters a message about Jesus and the need to be born again. Jesus himself, he insisted, would be totally opposed to any such attempts. In this clergyman's view, our only responsibility to human beings is Christian presence, to demonstrate the compassion of Jesus, which "will awaken in them their own spirituality."

Some on the proclamation side have argued that, while acts of service, mercy and justice are fruits of Christian commitment, they are not part of the church's mission. Thus, as one put it, "Historically the mission of the church is evangelism alone."[4] Others have said that both proclamation and presence are important, but we must begin with presence in order to gain a hearing for the gospel or as a way to make authentic the Christian message. In this perspective the divide is more logistical than theological.

A faith of the hands needs both proclamation and presence. They go together, and though different, they should not be pulled apart. Gifts and immediate situations may, of course, lead a person or church to focus on one side or the other at a given time, but overall we must be committed to both. Mission does not describe everything believers or the church does. Rather, as John Stott has put it, "Mission describes . . . everything the church is sent into the world to do. Mission embraces the church's double vocation of service to be 'the salt of the earth' and 'the light of the world.'"[5]

ACTIONS OF PROCLAMATION

The good news of Christ, the gospel, only makes sense in the context of the larger biblical story of creation, Fall, redemption and consummation that we described in chapter two. We really can see why Jesus died and why he has any claim on our lives only when we understand that God is the sovereign Creator of the universe, that humans are alienated from God, that God loves us and wants us to come back into harmony with him.

By its very nature the Christian worldview implies proclamation. While the living out of the ways of Christ and his kingdom is absolutely integral to our calling in this world, the human race could not know the meaning of Christ and the plan of God by actions alone. There is content to both the Christian worldview and the gospel itself. As the apostle Paul put it,

> How are they to call on one in whom they have not believed? And how are they to believe in one of whom they have never heard? And how are they to hear without someone to proclaim him? And how are they to proclaim him unless they are sent. As it is written, "How beautiful are the feet of those who bring good news!" (Rom 10:14-15)

Rachel, one of my former seminary students, one day shared her personal story with me. She had grown up in a church-going home and was in church most Sundays. Her congregation was involved in various social and economic ministries to the community. Growing up, Rachel saw good actions but felt that she had never clearly heard the message of the gospel. In retrospect she recognizes that it was there in the liturgy, but the gospel of Christ was never presented in a way that she realized the need to personally appropriate it. Fortunately, when Rachel went to university, she was befriended by a caring Christian who not only walked the walk but also shared her own personal journey to Christ. When Rachel heard its simple meaning, she was ecstatic to receive the good news. Indeed, "How beautiful are the feet [or hands] of those who bring good news."

The biblical mandate for proclamation. Jesus was very clear about the need for proclamation. Among his last words on earth were, "All authority in heaven and on earth has been given to me. Go therefore and make disciples of all nations, baptizing them in the name of the Father and of the Son and of the Holy Spirit, and teaching them to obey everything that I have commanded you" (Mt 28:18-20). In making this statement, which is often called the Great Commission, Jesus is giving his disciples and the church for all time a clear "hands" responsibility that incorporates the verbal telling of the good news of Christ.

It is important to understand exactly what Jesus is saying here. We often put the emphasis on the *go*, but grammatically it is not an imperative, but rather a participle implying something like this: "As you are going, make disciples." The implication is that Christians will be a going people, whether in the daily routines of life or in the special calling to take the gospel to a specific context. The imperative in the text is to "make disciples of all nations [that is, peoples]." Our intention in verbally sharing the good news is not to gain converts, but to enable the emergence of true disciples of Christ who will love him with head, heart and hands. Making disciples entails a public confession through baptism and the teaching of those who respond in faith, that they may "obey everything that I have commanded you." Incidentally, all that Christ commanded includes love of neighbor, service and justice—the presence dimension of his mission.

In Acts 1 we have another statement of Jesus that focuses on proclamation. After his resurrection, Jesus is instructing his followers to remain in Jerusalem until the Holy Spirit comes on them in new power.
They ask whether this will be the time when Jesus restores the kingdom
to Israel, indicating that they are expecting a physical, political type of
kingdom. Up until his last minutes on earth, Jesus is attempting to re-
orient their thinking and expectations. He says, "It is not for you to know
the time or periods that the Father has set by his own authority. But you
will receive power when the Holy Spirit has come on you; and you will
be my witnesses in Jerusalem, in all Judea and Samaria, and to the ends
of the earth" (vv. 7-8).

Jesus is saying that his mission will be carried out, not through their
own wisdom and ingenuity, but through the supernatural power of the
Holy Spirit, who was about to come on them in a new and fresh way.
Through that power they will be witnesses, beginning where they are
and extending to the furthest reaches of the earth. Being a witness certainly would involve their lives and their actions, but a witness is essentially one who gives testimony to what he has seen and experienced, as
in a court of law. Word and deed must go together in a witness, for the
witness's words are only to be believed by virtue of what he does (actions) and who he is (character).

God's work and our work. Christ makes clear to his early followers
that ultimately this is not their work. It is primarily the work of God,
who chooses to use his followers as vehicles to proclaim the good
news of the kingdom. Throughout the book of Acts, the church ex-
pands because Christians were willing to give witness to what they
had encountered in Jesus of Nazareth. But the underlying assumption
of this cataclysmic explosion of the gospel in the first century is that
this is God's work.

Because it is God's mission, it is amazing that God has entrusted this
work of the hands to such confused, finite, halting human beings. Ron
Sider tells a parable to make this point. He invites us to an imaginary

conversation between Jesus and the archangel Gabriel after our Lord's ascension back to heaven:

> "Well, how did it go?" Gabriel asks Jesus. "Did you complete your mission and save the world?" "Well, yes and no," Jesus replies. "I modeled a godly life for about thirty years. I preached to a few thousand Jews in one corner of the Roman Empire. I died for the sins of the world and promised that those who believe in me will live forever. And I burst from the tomb on the third day to show my circle of 120 frightened followers that my life and story are God's way to save the whole world. Then I gave the Holy Spirit to those 120 and left them to finish the task."
>
> "You mean," Gabriel asks in amazement, "your whole plan to save the world depends on that ragtag bunch of fisherman, ex-prostitutes, and tax collectors?" "That's right," Jesus replies.
>
> "But what if they fail?" Gabriel persists with growing alarm. "What's your back-up plan?"
>
> "There is no back-up plan," Jesus says quietly.[6]

God's whole mission of both proclamation and presence has been entrusted to us. The consolation is that despite our foibles this is God's mission, and the Spirit of God is with us.

Yet, this proclamation of the gospel is not a burden placed on us. Instead it is an eruption of joy fueled by the work of God through Christ on our behalf. It is such good news that it cannot be suppressed. The late Lesslie Newbigin, a noted mission leader for many years, put it well: "So the logic of mission is this: the true meaning of the human story has been disclosed. Because it is the truth, it must be shared universally. It cannot be private opinion."[7]

ACTIONS OF PRESENCE

When we explore the life of Jesus, we find word and deed, proclamation and presence. They needed each other in his ministry, and they need each other in ours as well. Christian presence is very simply the actions of believers in everyday life, demonstrating the Christ within them. In reality we not only proclaim a message, but are an actual part of the message. We are "a letter of Christ . . . written not with ink but with the Spirit of the living God" (2 Cor 3:3). What people often hear is what they see in us. Of course presence is closely tied to our character, which is a dimension of our heart. But here the focus is on the outward actions through the body, so that faith is demonstrated in what we do and how we live.

In earlier chapters we noted that the head and the heart are involved in conversion. We cannot truly believe unless both are involved. When we come to the hands we may want to say that there is something different. Faith is demonstrated through the hands, but the hands are not part of the faith or believing process. In part that is correct. We are not reconciled to God through action. But it is equally true that if deeds are not present, then we do not have genuine faith.

Ephesians 2 makes it quite clear that salvation is not acquired by human efforts: "For by grace you have been saved through faith, and this is not your own doing; it is the gift of God—not the result of works, so that no one may boast" (vv. 8-9). But the very next verse tells us that "we are what he has made us, created in Christ Jesus for good works, which God prepared beforehand to be our way of life" (v. 10). We were literally created by God to demonstrate in our lives the goodness and righteousness of God himself. While Christian presence does not earn salvation, there is no salvation without it.

The concrete reality of this truth is seen in the very next verses as Paul goes on to tackle one of the first social ethic issues with which the church had to wrestle. Jews and Gentiles were coming into the body of Christ through God's grace and bringing with them a long history of hostilities as well as very different cultural practices. How were they to live in the same body? The very first deed, or work, to be manifest was overcoming old social, cultural and historical barriers. Christ "is our peace; in his flesh he has made both groups into one and has broken down the dividing wall, that is, the hostility between us" (Eph 2:14). He has made in "himself one new humanity in place of the two, thus making peace, and might reconcile both groups to God in one body through the cross, thus putting to death that hostility through it" (Eph 2:15-16).

This is a classic text on justification by faith as opposed to works. But we miss much of the teaching here unless we recognize that God's work of grace within a person, if it is authentic, will always demonstrate itself. True saving faith will always show itself in Christian presence.

Jesus himself indicated this with reference to the scribes and Pharisees. In speaking of the importance of keeping God's law, he said, "I tell you, unless your righteousness exceeds that of the scribes and Pharisees, you will never enter the kingdom of heaven" (Mt 5:20). Jesus' point is not that we gain salvation by our own righteousness, but rather that God's saving righteousness in us through Christ must manifest itself in acts of righteousness. Otherwise faith is not real.

Other New Testament writers echo the same. James said:

> What good is it, my brothers and sisters, if you say you have faith but do not have works? Can faith save you? If a brother or sister is naked and lacks daily food, and one of you says to them, "Go in peace; keep warm and eat your fill," and yet you do not supply their bodily needs, what is the good of that? So faith by itself, if it has no works, is dead. (2:14-17)

In his first epistle, John similarly emphasized that one who continually sins does not abide in God's love, but conversely one who loves in truth and in action shows that they are in God's truth. Moreover, he asks, "How does God's love abide in anyone who has the world's goods and sees a brother or sister in need and yet refuses help?" (3:17). Thus "whoever does not love does not know God, for God is love" (4:8).

True saving faith in Christ will always be demonstrated, not because the deeds save us, but because deeds demonstrate the reality of Christ within. If the hands are missing in the overall configuration of one's life, then there is reason to ask whether faith in Christ as Savior and Lord is actually present.

Presence in everyday life. In the face of great challenges, human beings often readily rise to the occasion with acts of kindness and consideration toward others. In August of 2003 a power outage hit much of the East Coast and essentially created a standstill in New York City. Reminiscent of the terrorist attack of September 11, 2001, New Yorkers banded together in helping each other get home, finding overnight accommodations for stranded people and creating an atmosphere of cooperation and civility. There was virtually no looting. News reporters showed millions of people responding to a significant challenge and inconvenience with grace, patience and acts of compassion. For a moment one's faith in humanity was restored.

But it is one thing to act in noble ways in the face of tragedy, crisis and regional or national challenge. It is quite another to live daily with the same virtues. The call of Christian presence is not for heroic actions when the lights go out (figuratively and in reality), but for daily actions that show that Christ is within us. It is quite easy to love the world in the abstract or in the moment of dire need. It is quite another to daily love those who are closest to us.

Love is the chief virtue of faith from the perspective of character within the heart, and it is the "greatest of these" from the standpoint of human actions. Because God is love, God's own love within us—through redemption in Christ and the power of the Holy Spirit—is to be the key marker of Christian daily life. The way we treat one another in the family, the patient response to the ornery coworker, the grace with which we respond to the insecure neighbor and the caring hand to the overly dependent church member are the kinds of daily actions to which God calls us.

In 1 Corinthians 13, the great love chapter, Paul reminds us that we can have great heroic acts, such as giving away all our possessions, but without love we are nothing. The chapter goes on to describe what love looks like in the daily grind where the rubber meets the road: "Love is patient; love is kind; love is not envious or boastful or arrogant or rude. It does not insist on its own way; it is not irritable or resentful; it does not rejoice in wrongdoing, but rejoices in the truth. It bears all things, believes all things, hopes all things, endures all things" (vv. 4-7).

Along with love in daily life, there are other actions that reflect Christ-likeness. One of the most significant listings is the fruit of the Holy Spirit, some of which are internal virtues and others external actions: "love, joy, peace, patience, kindness, generosity, faithfulness, gentleness, and self-control" (Gal 5:22).

Failing to live out what we proclaim has been one of the greatest detriments to the Christian gospel. From the perspective of nonbelievers, the failure of the hands is likely far more significant than what happens in the head and the heart. And the failure has often come in the daily routines, not the heroic efforts. Dr. Sarvepalli Radhakrishnan was a Hindu philosopher and the former president of India. He had much exposure to Christianity and even graduated from a Christian university in south India. But Radhakrishnan never became a Christian. In fact he is said to have commented to some Christians in his country: "You claim that Jesus Christ is your Savior, but you do not appear to be more 'saved' than anyone else."[8] Mahatma Gandhi was a great admirer of Jesus, but in similar fashion he too rejected Jesus as Savior and Lord because of the failure of Christians to live out the message in which they claimed to believe.

The greatest challenge for a faith of the hands is to put it into practice in the realities of everyday life.

Presence in ethical actions. In a complex world, we face a host of ethical dilemmas. Medicine, law, politics, education, science, the arts, social work, business, sports and the environment all present us today with a host of complicated ethical issues. As noted in the previous chapter, Christian character is essential to these ethical challenges. But we cannot stop with character. In the rough and tumble of societal and cultural life, we are called by God to make good choices that are a sign of the Christian character formed within our hearts.[9]

People facing ethical choices make their decisions in multiple ways. Some appeal to conventionality (the way things are done), others to

principles (whether derived from reason or revelation) and still others to
a weighing of consequences. But ultimately people make their ethical
decisions in light of their worldview. Thus decisions that humans make
often reflect the particular worldview that guides their overall pattern of
thinking. In contemporary Western cultures the worldview is increasingly naturalistic with a tinge of spirituality: what I like to term spiritualistic naturalism. It is often coupled with a form of ethical decision-
making called utilitarianism, which calculates the greatest good for the
greatest number of people. The upshot of this worldview and ethical approach is a tendency toward relativism, which repudiates moral universals and absolutes.

A good example of this coalescence of spiritualistic naturalism and
utilitarianism can be seen in the recent push for euthanasia. Under the
guise of being compassionate and caring, this worldview grants humans the privilege to do with their lives as they see fit. Utilitarianism
says that if euthanasia results in less pain for a patient and greater ease
for family and friends, then it must be ethical. The relativism implicit
in these perspectives means that there are no givens, such as the sanctity of human life, that preclude taking life into our own hands when
it becomes burdensome.

In contrast, a Christian ethic is rooted in a Christian worldview, with
the understanding that there are moral universals that guide our path.
Thus, on the issue of euthanasia, human life is not ours to do with as we
please. Moreover, human dignity does not reside in our capacities or our
mental and physical condition, but rather inheres within us as bearers of
God's image. These givens preclude humans from taking the life of another or their own life, simply because it is burdensome or painful.

But a Christian ethic must do more than contend for ethical principles
and worldview guidelines. Believers must also act consistently with their
ethical commitments so rationales for unethical actions are undermined.
Take again the issue of euthanasia. Of course believers need to proclaim
their ethical convictions on this issue in the midst of a secular, pluralistic

world. But they also need to act with compassion, grace and Christian presence in the midst of human suffering and in the face of death. The best deterrent to euthanasia is a community of care that lives out its ethic, thus responding to pain and death with an alternate strategy.

Presence in social justice and righteousness. Closely related to ethical commitments and actions, Christian presence must also be displayed in the significant social justice issues. All societies experience the reality of sin, not only in the character and actions of individuals, but also in their social and cultural fabric. Thus most societies in some manner experience an assortment of sins, such as racism, ethnocentrism, economic injustice, political oppression, environmental degradation, gender exploitation and legal unrighteousness. Here the issues are not just those we face personally in our jobs and communities, but rather the broader issues that confront an entire society. They are social or institutional sins.

When I pastored in Washington, D.C., one of my parishioners was Gary Haugen, the founder and president of International Justice Mission. While an undergraduate at Harvard, Haugen became convinced that the gospel needed to be proclaimed as truth and lived out in the hurts and injustices of the world. After graduating from the University of Chicago Law School, he went to work for the U.S. Department of Justice as a trial attorney in the Civil Rights Division. In 1994, he was seconded to the United Nations to serve as the Officer in Charge of the UN's genocide investigation in Rwanda. Through these experiences he became convinced that Christians needed to be at the forefront in using legal skills to defend biblical justice for the powerless and abused of the world. With his highly specialized skills and education, he gathered a group of like-minded Christians to begin International Justice Mission.

International Justice Mission (IJM) is working around the world, pursuing justice for the oppressed using two main approaches: casework and education. In casework their legal professionals use legal expertise, investigative strategies and cutting-edge technologies to rescue victims of injustice in areas such as bonded slavery, illegal detention and sex trafficking of children. Their mission: "Through its education initiatives, IJM provides people of faith with the training, mobilization tools and resources to translate their convictions into active engagement."[10] Their work has helped to prevent a corrupt judge from gaining a seat on the Supreme Court of Honduras. Through contacts with World Vision workers, IJM was able to convince the police to make an arrest of a man who had raped a mentally handicapped girl, but was allowed by police and officials to roam free. Haugen's vision and IJM's mission is making a difference in the world, flowing from a deep biblical commitment to the gospel and social justice.

Christians believe that the foundational solution to all social and cultural ills resides in the redemptive work of Christ, which will be consummated in his coming kingdom. There is no Utopia this side of glory. But Christ calls us to live now as signs of that coming kingdom. Thus we are called to engage the social and cultural issues of our time, not out of an ideological or politicized perspective, but from within the framework of our biblical worldview. That engagement is not an attempt to rule the world, but rather a divine calling to carry out God's cultural mandate to be "salt and light" within the world.

The metaphors used by Jesus to describe our role in society are highly significant. In the Sermon on the Mount he called his followers "the salt of the earth" and "the light of the world" (Mt 5:13-14). Salt in that day was a preservative agent, thus Jesus is connoting a role in limiting the world's injustice and unrighteousness. Light is a medium of guidance and illumination, thus suggesting a role in helping give direction in the midst of the social and cultural problems. Another metaphor Jesus employed was leaven, connoting the influence that a small ingredient can have for achieving good.

These metaphors certainly embody both proclamation and presence, but none of them imply a dominance of Christians over society. The biblical assumption is that Christians are attempting to be a Christian presence as aliens in a foreign land. In the midst of a secular, pluralistic culture we will need, like Israel long ago during the Babylonian captivity, to learn to "sing the LORD's song in a foreign land" (Ps 137:4).

How will we do this? Approaches to being salt, light and leaven will vary among Christians. IJM's strategies are just one approach. It is important to remember that there are differences between the principles or norms that guide our social action and the strategies employed to carry them out. For example, we should agree that creation in the image of God and principles of justice and love preclude racism and ethnocentrism. Those are biblical absolutes on which we cannot waver. But we may disagree on the strategies or technical solutions to best achieve justice and human rights in race and ethnic relations in a given society. The same is true for most social problems, whether they be related to economics, medicine, law or the environment. Sadly in our culture today there is a tendency to relativize the moral norms and absolutize the strategies. This reveals the deep confusion of a culture that has lost its way in dealing with the great social/cultural problems of our age.

As Christians engage these ills, we need clear understanding of the nature of the problems. Part of the success of IJM is a clear understanding of the nature of law and the issues being addressed. Superficial renditions and ideological enslavements will be counterproductive in Christian social presence. There is a great need for Christians to enter every domain of societal and cultural life, not to take over the world by fallen, "worldly" means, but rather to be salt, light and leaven with reference to the issues of our time. Such a faith of the hands should always incorporate the head to understand both the norms that guide us and the realities that confront us. And such a faith should always incorporate the heart to motivate and sustain our commitments and actions, which will often go against the stream of the prevailing social and cultural norms.

INCARNATIONAL SERVANTHOOD

Christian proclamation and Christian presence ought to go together, and in fact they have their most powerful impact in tandem. Together they reflect the incarnation of Christ, who took on flesh and lived in the midst of a world that needed his love, justice and redemption. Word and deed always follow the example of Christ's incarnational servanthood, for "the Son of Man came not to be served but to serve, and to give his life a ransom for many" (Mk 10:45).

Wayne Gordon, a pastor in one of the poorest and most violent areas of Chicago, is a wonderful example of a faith of the hands, bringing proclamation and presence together. Soon after his conversion as a teenager, Gordon looked into the face of God and promised, "I will do anything that you want me to do with my life." He therefore defied roaches, break-ins and violence to tell inner-city kids—with virtually no hope of a decent education, job or marriage—that the Creator of the universe loves them and wants them to live with him eternally. Because he followed Jesus' example of caring for the whole person, he also started tutoring programs, recreational services, a health clinic, a job training facility, low-income housing and small businesses. After twenty years, God has blessed Gordon's faith, prayer and hard work with a thriving, interracial church of five hundred people and a vast, holistic, multimillion-dollar community center that is transforming one of the most devastated sections of Chicago.[11]

We may not all be called to the heart of the inner city like Wayne Gordon. But we are called to a faith of the hands that both proclaims and lives out in actions the good news of Jesus Christ.

DISCUSSION QUESTIONS

1. Why is the body so important to the Christian faith? What have you observed about Christians' attitudes toward the body? How is the body linked to faith expressed with the hands?

2. What have been your observations about the divide between proclamation and presence? Why have believers and the church had a difficult time holding them together? What can be done to help hold them together?

3. Study Matthew 28:18-20 and Acts 1:1-8. What do these passages teach us about the importance of evangelism? What do they teach us about how evangelism should be done? Why is evangelism so hard in our age?

4. Study Ephesians 2:8-15. What does this passage tell us about the nature of Christian presence? Which aspects of Christian presence do you find the hardest to implement? Are there other dimensions of Christian presence that you believe are significant for being the "hands" and "feet" of Jesus?

7

DISTORTIONS OF THE HANDS

In the opening chapter we met Jeff, the thoughtful Christian who had a ready answer for the questions to his faith. Jeff knew the Bible, theology and apologetics with a thoroughness that was the envy of his friends and colleagues. But as Jeff lived his faith, it was almost entirely through the categories of the mind.

To be sure, Jeff's faith expression in one sense had a bit of hands orientation, for he used his knowledge to defend the faith and refute rival worldviews. But his approach to Christianity was in reality a distortion of the hands in two ways. First, he perceived witness to be primarily focused on winning rational arguments. Many who listened to him did not experience his head-oriented witness to be consistent with the love of Christ, as argumentation seemed to take precedence over the real needs of people. Second, Jeff had a minimal emphasis on Christian presence. In fact he often chided those who were committed to justice and service, as if they distorted the core of the gospel. For Jeff the faith was primarily beliefs that one shared and defended.

We also met Jennifer, the social activist; she was the kind of person Jeff believed would lead us astray. Jennifer's problem was the opposite of

Jeff's, for she boiled the faith down primarily to actions. She was not guided by theology or biblical studies as grounding for her action. She was not motivated and sustained by a heart that was focused on the presence and power of Christ in her life. As Jennifer saw it, the Christian faith was primarily about the hands—actions of justice and mercy for the injustices and hurts of the world.

Both Jeff and Jennifer represent distortions of the hands—the one from neglect, the other from overemphasis. In this chapter we explore what happens when these kinds of distortions appear. As in the other distortion chapters, we will conclude by examining the ways we can nurture the hands for the glory of God.

WHEN ACTION IS NEGLECTED

What happens if Christians and the church neglect the hands? What becomes of faith that is devoid of proclamation and presence? As with the head and the heart, the consequences are significant.

A dead faith. A faith without action is a dead faith. As James put it, "What good is it, my brothers and sisters, if you say you have faith but do not have works? Can faith save you? If a brother or sister is naked and lacks daily food, and one of you says to them, 'Go in peace . . . ,' and yet does not supply their bodily needs, what is the good of that? So faith by itself, if it has no works, is dead" (2:14-17). The teaching of this and similar passages seems to be that such alleged faith is not real or genuine faith. That is, if one has right beliefs and right affections and feelings, but does not demonstrate them in action, there is good reason to question that faith. Of course, and fortunately, we are not the ones who have to make that judgment. But as a general principle we must affirm what Scripture affirms: faith without works is dead or lifeless, not genuine faith.

It is dead not only from the standpoint of a person's own spiritual existence, but also dead in terms of its impact on others. When action is neglected, God's work in the world is hampered. As we saw in the previous chapter with Ryan and Susan, a "Christianity" without genuine Christian action frequently leads to the charge of hypocrisy. And hypocrisy is typically the number-one reason unbelievers give for not coming to Christ. Hypocrisy is found not only in the lives of individuals, but also in the collective body, the church, when it fails to outwardly express the reality of the Christ it confesses.

God's design is that we carry out the sacred task of his mission to the world, despite our sin and finitude. We are significant beings in God's eyes and thus have been given "the ministry of reconciliation" (2 Cor 5:18), a ministry of both proclamation (verbally sharing the message of reconciliation in Christ) and presence (reconciliation of peoples who have been alienated from each other). The ultimate work of reconciliation belongs to Christ, but "we are ambassadors for Christ, since God is making his appeal through us" (2 Cor 5:20).

Thus individual Christians and the church are indicted when they fail to carry out ministries of the hands. God has established his world in such a way that humans are to bear responsibility, and his world is negatively impacted when they fail to carry it out. Therefore when the white church in South Africa for most of the twentieth century went along with subjugating fellow citizens in an unjust apartheid system, it thwarted the work of God in that country and around the world. And when "Christians" in North America live lifestyles of apathetic affluence without regard to the physical needs of others in the world, it thwarts the work of the gospel. Of course God is never limited by his creatures or his church; God is far greater than that. But our Maker has established the church to be the primary place through which people can see Jesus and the work of God's kingdom. When the church and individual Christians do not live up to their calling, the world suffers. It is a dead faith.

Impact on our thinking. We are quite at home with the idea that distorted thinking leads to distorted living. We are less at home with the idea that distorted living can lead to distorted thinking. But just as Christians can get their lives wrong because they got their theology wrong, so

"Christians often get their theology wrong because they got their lives wrong,"[1] according to theologian Stanley Hauerwas. Because we are whole beings it goes both ways. Thus the way we think is often significantly influenced by our actions. Good actions can have a positive effect on our theology, and distorted actions can negatively affect our theology.

To put it another way, we do not really know until we do, and we learn as we do. As Paul stated in Colossians 1:9-10, "We have not ceased praying for you and asking that you may be filled with the knowledge of God's will in all spiritual wisdom and understanding, so that you may lead lives worthy of the Lord, fully pleasing to him, as you bear fruit in every good work and as you grow in the knowledge of God." The pattern here is knowledge . . . action . . . knowledge.

As an example of the positive impact actions can have on our theology, take the issue of evangelism. One of the best ways to bolster our belief in the power of Christ as our divine Savior and Lord is through actively sharing our faith and then seeing people come to Christ. I will never forget the reinforcement in my theology when my friend Brian came to faith during my pastoral ministry in Washington, D.C. Over the years friends had frequently shared their faith in Christ with Brian, but it almost appeared that he didn't need salvation. After all, he had so much of his life together, had high moral standards—and a nicer person you couldn't find.

I met with Brian numerous times to discuss readings and the tough issues surrounding Christian faith. Throughout this long process of several years, I found myself beginning to doubt the power of the gospel and the relevance of Jesus. Does a person like Brian really need Christ? Does the gospel have anything to really offer to people whose lives are essentially together? But as I and others continued to share by word and by deed, the fruit of our labors paid off and he eventually made his decision for Christ. Brian's conversion had a deep impact on me personally, particularly solidifying my own deep conviction that Jesus is indeed the eternal Son of God and that salvation through him is necessary.

Conversely, there can be a negative impact on theology for those who never personally engage in a faith of the hands through proclamation. A person's theology of Christ and of salvation can be stunted if she never experiences and observes the transformations that come when people encounter Christ. It is easy to then view Christ as a great model or a good teacher and salvation as a process of changing the world through human efforts or a process of "humanization." The bottom line is that our actions and experiences in sharing Christ, or in not sharing Christ, can significantly impact our theological commitments.

Or take the example of forgiveness. While we are to forgive our enemies because of God's forgiveness through Christ, our forgiving of others in the midst of life's conflicts and hurts enables us to be more sensitive to the forgiveness of God and enables us to more fully grasp its implications. We become more open to divine forgiveness when we see and experience human forgiveness, just as we come to see the true meaning of human forgiveness when we experience God's forgiveness. In the Bible there is an intimate relationship between divine forgiveness and human forgiveness, as evidenced in the Lord's Prayer: "Forgive us our debts, as we also have forgiven our debtors" (Mt 6:12).

In Matthew 18 Jesus tells the story of the unmerciful servant, who is forgiven of a great debt but cannot forgive one who owes him a very small debt. The wicked servant receives judgment. Jesus concludes the story with these words: "So my heavenly Father will also do to every one of you, if you do not forgive our brother or sister from your heart" (v. 35). Jesus is teaching that true divine forgiveness will be demonstrated in human forgiveness. But he is also implying that if we do not forgive others when they have wronged us, we have not comprehended divine forgiveness. Our actions in forgiving others or failing to forgive others will always be intimately connected to our theological understanding of God's forgiveness in Jesus Christ.

Or take what happens theologically when acts of service, mercy and justice are missing. The failure to incorporate such actions into the Christian life negatively impacts our theological anthropology—our view of humanity. Essentially, failing to embody actions of presence leads to a disembodied anthropology in which we tend to view humans as mere souls. Acts of service, mercy and justice should focus on the real needs of real people in real places. Through these actions we are reminded that we can never reduce a human being to a mere soul that needs to be saved, but rather are ministering to a whole person with spiritual, physical, emotional and social needs. Without such actions our theological thinking is readily distorted.

Because we are whole beings with head, heart and hands intimately related, our actions really can influence our theology. Thus actions of piety (like prayer), justice, mercy and proclamation of the gospel all play a role in helping us to understand the nature, ways and purposes of God. Seeing God at work, even through finite, fallen human vessels, can have a significant impact on our theology. As Ellen Charry, a theologian at Princeton Seminary, puts it, "Separating thought from action is dangerous. They are interdependent, each one necessary to enrich and correct the other. Separated, thought withers and action decays."[2]

Impact on the sentiments of our heart. A faith without the hands also impacts the heart. Our will, affections, feelings and deep-seated understandings are all affected by our actions. And when right actions are missing, the sentiments of our heart fall short of God's intentions.

A good example of this is love. Love is both action and affection. Obviously, when our affections toward another reflect a selfless inner drive for that person's good, it will be demonstrated in actions of goodness toward that person. But our actions of goodness also create even greater affection toward the person we love. Those of us who are married know that this happens all the time. We may not always feel love within our heart toward our spouse in the midst of everyday pressures and responsibilities, but when we take the time to show acts of kindness and love, it actually strengthens our inner love. Without actions of love our heart grows cold. Thus at times we act our way into our feelings just as we act our way into our thinking.

This is also true at the social level with issues of justice. Our hearts are often moved toward justice and mercy when we become involved in acts of justice and mercy in the real world. In turn, these actions can engender even greater sentiments toward real needs. Charles Finney, the nineteenth-century revivalist and abolitionist, clearly understood this. In his *Lectures on Revivals of Religion* he contended that "revivals are hindered when ministers and churches take wrong ground in regard to any question involving human rights." He was particularly addressing the "sin" of slavery and noted, "One of the reasons for the low state of religion at the present time, is that many churches have taken the wrong side on the subject of slavery."[3] Today we often lack the will toward and affections of justice, compassion and mercy because the actions are missing, and in turn this hinders our affection toward God. A handless faith will dull the heart.

WHEN ACTIONS ARE SUPREME

Though the hands are essential to authentic Christian faith, we cannot live by hands alone. A faith of action without head and heart has been attempted often throughout the history of the church. The results are always wanting.

Self-sufficiency (works righteousness). A faith focused exclusively or primarily on the hands often leads to a sense of personal self-sufficiency. When we are engaged in the world without divine guidance and empowerment, we look within ourselves for both the direction our actions should take and the motivations for those actions. We easily come to believe that we (individually or corporately) have the resources to do God's work in the world. This sense of self-sufficiency reflects human pride, which many have taken to be the original sin.

Self-sufficiency in human action is really a form of works righteousness. Martin Luther, the great sixteenth-century Protestant reformer, was a formative catalyst in reminding the church that we are not saved by our own works, but by God's grace. Luther understood this not only with reference to salvation, but also in relation to actions resulting from faith. Just as it is possible to bank on our own deeds to come to God, so it is possible to bank on our own actions in reflecting and living out our faith. But as Luther so powerfully reminded us, our salvation and our sanctification are by God's grace. In other words, an imbalanced faith focused primarily on action will throw us back on ourselves as the primary resource for acts of righteousness.

The result of hands-only works righteousness is that people often grow weary in doing good. Many movements addressing social ills have been short-lived because people burned out for the cause. Thrown back on their own resources, they lacked suprahuman power and insight for maintaining their commitments and actions.

Superficial faith. A faith focused primarily on action also has a propensity to produce superficiality. Whether the activism is focused on deeds (presence) or on evangelism (proclamation), this brand of Christianity usually ends up with such a strong commitment to relevance that a deep and profound faith is lacking. Action without theology and spirituality breeds a "light faith," which lacks the ability to weather the intellectual, cultural or personal storms of life.

In American Christianity this superficiality of activism has at times been driven by pragmatism. Americans are a pragmatic people who accept the creed "Whatever works must be true; and whatever is true must work." Pragmatism has often been an impetus behind social activist movements of the religious left and the religious right, as both movements have followed the ideological cultural winds to gain adherents to the cause. If a given ideology seems to work and move the masses, it is deemed to be good and true. Rather than being rooted in the hard work of theological reflection and a reliance on the empowerment of God's Spirit, some Christian social activists have been drawn to what works, not to what is true, just, good and right.

The pragmatism of American culture has sometimes opened the way for an uncritical embrace of marketing as the means of doing God's work in the world. This has particularly been a tendency in recent decades within the church growth movement and certain forms of evangelism. Some quarters have begun to believe that if a particular method works in gaining adherents to the faith it must be blessed by God. No scrutiny or questions need be asked. Os Guinness, an evangelical who writes broadly on the intersection of faith and culture, has critiqued this approach as a cultural captivity. He notes that one Christian advertising agent, who represented the Coca-Cola Company and marketed the "I Found It" evangelistic campaign, paraded his golden calf blatantly: "Back in Jerusalem where the church started, God performed a miracle there on the day of Pentecost. They didn't have the benefits of buttons and media, so God had to do a little supernatural work there. But today, with our technology, we have available to us the opportunity to create the same kind of interest in a secular society."[4]

Of course this is one of the brasher examples of marketing and pragmatism in evangelism, but softer examples abound on the American landscape. The result is a superficial kind of religiosity that fails to do justice to either the Bible or the realities of life that humans encounter. Such "witness" to the world bears more the marks of the world itself than the marks of the Word it seeks to spread. And when depth of head and heart are missing, a focus primarily on action tends to move toward heterodoxy.

Heterodox faith. We have already seen that a faith of the head or the heart alone can lead to theological understandings that are contrary to Scripture and to historic understandings in the Christian church. The same is true for the hands. To bank on actions alone can lead to theological aberrations.

Take the issue of a theology of marriage and divorce. When John and Stephanie were married, they were deeply committed to the view that marriage is a sacred vow, intended for life. They truly believed that good families are vital to the health of society. After fifteen years of marriage and three children, John and Stephanie found themselves drifting apart. Their jobs were all-encompassing, and they rarely spent time with and for each other. Conflicts emerged, hurt engulfed the relationship, and they decided to divorce.

When their pastor reminded them of the covenant they had made on their wedding day, John and Stephanie waved it off with an appeal to their personal needs, incompatibility and the impossibility of mending the hurts. They even indicated that they believed divorce was legitimate if two people were no longer able to make things work and their emotional needs were not met. Years after the divorce had taken place John and Stephanie still held that belief. Their actions had led to a change in their theology; in this case clearly as a justification of their actions. What John and Stephanie experienced can often be observed in persons going through divorce, as their actions lead to a change in their beliefs about marriage and divorce.[5] On this issue the church in many quarters has moved away from biblical and traditional understandings, to the detriment of church and society.

Heterodox formulations have also at times emerged in individuals and groups that focus almost exclusively on social action. When actions of justice, peace or service become the defining character of Christianity, core elements of Christian faith are frequently diminished. Belief in a transcendent God who is providentially at work in history gives way to a temporal God who comes alongside human efforts and visions. Belief about the necessity of personal salvation through God's grace and faith in Christ gives way to human renovation of culture and society. Belief about the Bible as God's Word and the authority for life and thought gives way to human insights of sociology and psychology. Belief about a coming kingdom of God gives way to a new social order designed by humanity, with the aid of God.

Jennifer, our social activist from the opening of the book and this chapter, grew up believing that Jesus was the eternal Son of God, who became incarnate, died for the sins of the world, rose again from the dead and is the only means of salvation. As Jennifer began to focus exclusively on a faith of the hands (of the presence variety) her theology shifted. On a visit home with an old friend she confided, "I just no longer believe that salvation through Christ is the greatest need of humanity. In fact I sometimes wonder if Jesus wasn't just a great prophet and teacher, with incredible insights into human need. To me Easter is a celebration of the kind of 'resurrection' we can anticipate in bringing change to the injustices of this world."

We must be aware that, while actions of justice and mercy are necessary for authentic Christianity, actions of justice and mercy dislodged from theology, transcendence and a heart for God usually lead to a distorted faith. The records of history tell the story.

Misuses of proclamation. Most of the above descriptions are related to actions of mercy and justice. But there is another distortion sometimes found among those with an imbalanced zeal for proclaiming the gospel. Evangelism does not always sit well with some people. In part this may occur because one is ashamed of the gospel (see Rom 1:16), but it also occurs because of the way evangelism has been carried out.

Greg was thirty-five years old when he became a believer. He had grown up in a church but said he had no sense of what it meant to truly believe in and follow Christ. He dropped out of church after high school and showed little interest in spiritual realities. Through the witness of people at work he eventually came to Christ. His life was radically transformed, and as is often true of new converts he was eager to share his newfound faith with others. Greg was an intense person and he brought that intensity to his witness. Furthermore he was somewhat dismayed that throughout all his years he never had been challenged with the claims of Christ, not even by the church of his childhood.

As a result Greg began buttonholing people at work on company time. He wanted others to experience what he had experienced, but he often lacked tact and respect for others in his witness. Whenever he got together with his extended family, Greg was in their faces with the gospel. As a result both family and coworkers began to pull away from him out of discomfort. Some believers tried to remind him that the method of sharing the gospel ought to be congruent with Christ's love, but Greg felt that rejection was the cost of being a true believer. In the end he alienated many and won over few.

Greg's story is a good reminder that how we do proclamation must be consistent with the spirit of Christ and the nature of the gospel itself. Commitment to truth must always be accompanied by commitment to love. One without the other leads to a distorted faith.

Such distortions are nothing new, for they were already present in the early church. Paul wrote, "For we are not peddlers of God's word like so many; but in Christ we speak as persons of sincerity, as persons sent from God and standing in his presence" (2 Cor 2:17). The "peddlers" were hawkers of the gospel who carried out their ministry as if the Christian message was some kind of merchandise, which could be sold by unscrupulous methods. Such peddling or hawking is often driven by false motives: arrogance, pride of success or numbers, insecurity, or even judgmentalism. Triumphalism has often accompanied these distorted strategies, and with it have come cultural insensitivity and ideological baggage.

A helpful image for correcting these distortions has been suggested by Daniel Niles, a church leader from Sri Lanka: the image of a beggar. Evangelism, or proclamation, is a beggar telling other beggars where they could find food, and we are all beggars.[6] Such a spirit leaves no place for arrogance, cultural imperialism or triumphalism. It is a reminder that proclamation must always be accompanied by Christian presence—a lifestyle and actions that commend the gospel message.

NURTURING THE HANDS

In light of the distortions of the hands, we do well to think about how we can properly nurture Christian action. How can we grow the active side of life to be in balance with the mind and affections? And how can we engender a balance between acts of presence and proclamation?

Attention to the head and heart. It should be obvious by now that one of the keys to nurturing a life of action is giving attention to the head and the heart. Having a worldview that stresses the significance and role of proclamation and presence is a powerful impetus toward putting it into practice. And when our heart is bent in that direction we are more apt to do it. Our theology needs to reflect on what the gospel and a Christian worldview mean for the concrete realities of humans and society. And our inner spirituality needs to always be moving outward, not resting content on an inner peace, joy or transformation, which taken alone can turn into narcissism.

At the same time we also know that having right knowledge, and even a will or emotions directed toward good intentions, does not automatically produce actions of word and deed. Sometimes putting into practice what we believe and what we feel is difficult. Thus, along with attention to the mind and the heart, we can also nurture the hands in one other way: putting ourselves in the right places.

Putting ourselves in the right places. Putting ourselves into places of action is essential for becoming doers of the Word. One of the tendencies of Christians throughout various periods of history has been to isolate themselves from the world and its fallen ways. The motivation for this is laudable—to maintain a life of holiness or distinctiveness for the glory of God. But such isolation not only fails to carry out God's mandates for the church, it also tends to build a fortress mentality that only leads us further from the world to which God has called us.

To guard against this tendency we do well to intentionally place ourselves in places where we rub shoulders with unbelievers and have opportunity for ministries of proclamation and presence. Contacts and interactions can come through neighbors, coworkers, extended family members, professional colleagues and people we encounter in civic and community involvements. These settings offer appropriate opportunities to both live and share Christ, and both are necessary for authentic witness.

To become involved in the social, cultural and ethical issues of our day we will need to place ourselves into contexts in which we can legit-

imately play a role. Speaking from the sidelines, as the church has sometimes done, fails to engage the cultural and social realities in ways that
have integrity and can really make a difference. To be involved in the
simplest forms of service to the needs of humanity we will often have to
take the initiative, as individuals and churches, to place ourselves into
the settings where the needs exist. Making commitments to be involved
and having accountability structures that ensure our carrying through
on the commitments are vital to the process. Usually such commitments
require being fully engaged in the Christian community where our resolve to action is nurtured and accountability is maintained.

N. T. Wright, a British scholar and church leader, has summed up the
calling of Christian presence well:

> We need Christian people to work as healers: as healing judges and prison
> staff, as healing teachers and administrators, as healing shopkeepers and
> bankers, as healing musicians and artists, as healing writers and scientists,
> as healing diplomats and politicians. We need people who will hold on to
> Christ firmly with one hand and reach out with the other, with wit and
> skill and cheerfulness, with compassion and sorrow and tenderness, to
> the places where our world is in pain. We need people who will use all
> their God-given skills . . . to analyze where things have gone wrong, to
> come to the place of pain, and to hold over the wound the only medicine
> which will really heal, which is the love of Christ made incarnate once
> more, the strange love of God turned into your flesh and mine, your smile
> and mine, your tears and mine, . . . and your joy and mine.[7]

The incarnational life of action can make a difference in the world.
But it must always be truly incarnational: Christ's love flowing through
us to a world that desperately needs his love and redemption.

DISCUSSION QUESTIONS

1. What have your experiences been with Christian expressions that neglect authentic action? Have you observed other consequences than
   the three described in this chapter?

2. We are quite at home hearing that our beliefs influence our actions. How do you assess the contention that our actions influence our beliefs? What other ways have you seen action influence thinking?

3. What have your experiences been with an approach that makes actions supreme? Have you observed other consequences than those described in this chapter?

4. What are the greatest challenges for you in nurturing a faith of action? What are some of the ways you have activated and nurtured the hands?

8

HEAD, HEART AND
HANDS TOGETHER

The Biblical Case

I t was a wonderful three months that our family spent in India. Mary Ann and I were teaching at Union Biblical Seminary in Pune and quickly learned that, while we were there to serve, we were frequently the ones being served by Indian believers' spiritual vitality and understandings. We were introduced to new ideas and new people, present and past. One of the persons we learned of was Pandita Ramabai (1858-1922), who many consider to be one of the greatest reformers in India's history. We all have fond memories of our ox-cart ride from the train station to Mukti Mission, a home and school for girls founded by this remarkable woman.

Ramabai grew up in a devout Hindu home that was devoted to a quest for inward peace and spiritual reality. In contrast to the patterns of the day, her father taught her languages, history and the religious writings of Hinduism. Ramabai developed into a brilliant woman who eventually learned seven languages and could quote from memory eighteen thousand verses of the *Purana,* one of the Hindu sacred writings. But her hunger for spiritual reality continued, particularly fueled by the sordid social conditions of her society and especially the treatment of women.

It was out of a failed spiritual quest and the conditions of her own society that Ramabai eventually became a Christian while studying in England. She described her conversion this way: "I realized after reading the 4th Chapter of John's Gospel that Christ was truly the divine Savior He claimed to be, and no one but He could transform and uplift the downtrodden women of India. . . . Thus, my heart was drawn to the religion of Christ and I was intellectually convinced of its truth."[1]

After her conversion Pandita (a title of honor) Ramabai began to teach women, believing that they were as capable of learning as men. As an intellectual, she studied the Bible and her own culture and history, and brought it all together in the founding of an institution for abandoned and orphaned girls, desperate widows and the blind. The Mukti (meaning "salvation") Mission continues today as an orphanage for the neglected, schools with more than a thousand young people (including schooling for the blind), a large hospital treating thousands of needy Indians, homes for the unwanted (that is, widows, outcasts, unwed mothers and special-needs children) and one of the largest churches in India. Much of what exists today was fueled by a significant spiritual revival in 1905, which touched the hearts of Ramabai and hundreds of young women at the mission.

Why was Ramabai able to accomplish so much for Christ and her country? Of course there are various factors, but I believe that among them is the fact that she developed a faith of the head, heart and hands. Unlike many of the Western missionaries who sometimes criticized her work and methods, Ramabai understood that her faith involved intellectual beliefs, deep passions of the heart and actions of both proclamation and presence. When she read the Bible she saw things that some of the missionaries did not see, because of their Western bifurcations of thought, action and feeling. She saw that the whole person is converted and must be engaged in faithfulness to Christ.

In the preceding chapters I have attempted to show that a case can be made for the role of the head, heart and hands in Christian faith. But it is time now to go a step further and see the three together. Just as a symphony is not a symphony with instruments acting alone, so our lives are not truly human and truly Christian with head, heart and hands acting in seclusion from each other. It is in the joyous consort of our whole selves that we begin to reflect something of God's designs for the human race. And it is in the interpenetration of head, heart and hands that we begin to discover what it means to truly be a follower of Jesus Christ, as Ramabai learned, experienced and expressed.

Can a biblical case really be made for bringing head, heart and hands together so that one without the others is shown to be incomplete? I believe it can. Any contention for framing the Christian faith and life in a way that is less than familiar needs biblical support for its validity. The Bible, God's Word written, is our final arbiter for life and thought. As I have been reading the Bible in recent years I have grown increasingly aware of the appeals to all dimensions of our self, or what I have termed the head, heart and hands. Biblical calls for righteous living, inner piety, truthful thinking and authentic love of God and neighbor frequently bring together the mind, the inner self and the outward actions. What follows are just a few such passages from both the Old and New Testaments that bring these three dimensions together.

Old Testament

Deuteronomy 6:1-9.

> Now this is the commandment—the statutes and the ordinances—that the LORD your God charged me to teach you to observe in the land that you are about to cross into and occupy, so that you and your children and your children's children may fear the LORD your God. . . . Hear, O Israel: The LORD is our God, the LORD alone. You shall love the LORD your God with all your heart, and with all your soul, and with all your might. Keep these words that I am commanding you today in your heart. Recite them

to your children and talk about them when you are at home and when
you are away, when you lie down and when you rise. Bind them as a sign
on your hands, fix them as an emblem on your forehead, and write them
on the doorposts of your house and on your gates.

Likely given to Israel as they were soon to enter the Promised Land,
these words came to constitute the creed of Israel, eventually becoming
part of Jewish daily rituals. It is often referred to as the Shema, taken
from the opening Hebrew word. The heart is explicitly mentioned in the
text, but there is also clearly a theological focus encompassing the mind,
for the Shema "exclude[s] any concept of polytheism in Israel's God, for
he is not many but one. Above all, there is an exclusiveness about Yahweh which demands total love from his people."[2] To believe that God is
one involves the mind in an affirmation of thought, but draws on a commitment of the heart that will not assent to any other ultimate commitments in life. Moreover, in his summary of the Shema (Mt 22:37) Jesus
explicitly named the mind as part of loving God. This belief of the mind
and sentiments of the heart are evidenced in daily life by obeying and
observing God's commandments. And they are commandments that are
known, written, explicated and applied.

The Shema is a clear example of a holistic faith that brings the whole
of one's self together in the context of a community of believers. The rec-
itation of God's oneness and the commandments was to be bolstered by
symbolic and even ritualistic actions. The words would be found on the
doorposts, in the daily routines of life from morning to night, and they
would be etched in the fabric of the people's hearts. And yet the firmness
of heart could not exist without the theological affirmation that God is
one and the actions demonstrating that claim in the realities of everyday
life. Without the head, the claims about God's nature as one and exclusive are meaningless; without the heart, such claims are mere rhetoric;
without the hands, such claims and their corresponding laws have no
life and reality in everyday existence.

Proverbs 19:1-3.

Better the poor walking in integrity / than one perverse of speech who is a fool. / Desire without knowledge is not good, / and one who moves too hurriedly misses the way. / One's own folly leads to ruin, / yet the heart rages against the LORD.

These three verses constitute three separate proverbs, but they are tied together by at least one theme: the integration of head, heart and hands. The Proverbs are concrete, practical sayings that could be easily memorized in the mind, firmly implanted as virtues within the heart and visibly applied to daily living. The Hebrew people could not fathom one without the others. There was no sense that the proverb must first be understood, then believed in the heart and then acted on. Rather, the knowledge, understanding, sentiments, will and actions all flowed together into one whole. Thus, "walking in integrity," "desire without knowledge" and "the heart rages against the LORD" reflect an assumption that a person can only be faithful to Yahweh when thinking, affections and actions are walking in harmony, influencing and shaping each other.

Hosea 4:6-7.

My people are destroyed for lack of knowledge; / because you have rejected knowledge, / I reject you from being a priest to me. / And since you have forgotten the law of your God, / I also will forget your children. The more they increased, / the more they sinned against me; / they changed their glory into shame.

Written in the eighth century B.C. to the Northern Kingdom of Israel, the book of Hosea is a powerful prophetic witness against the sins, injustices and apathy of the people. The prophet is best remembered for taking the radical action of marrying a harlot and accepting her back despite her harlotry, to remind the Hebrew people of God's gracious offer of forgiveness despite their waywardness.

In this text Hosea appears to put the primary blame on knowledge.

But it must be remembered that knowledge in the Old Testament is never understood as a purely rational enterprise apart from the rest of the self. Indeed knowledge and understanding are frequently understood as functions of the heart. From the rest of the book it is clear that the knowledge of God and divine law are intimately related to inner sentiments. Moreover, a will that is hardened to God is intimately connected to unjust and unrighteous actions. Hosea's indictment earlier in the chapter is that "there is no faithfulness or loyalty, and no knowledge of God in the land" (4:1)—functions of heart and head. Intermeshed with this lack of inner loyalty and knowledge of God is this: "Swearing, lying, and murder, and stealing and adultery break out; bloodshed follows bloodshed. Therefore the land mourns" (4:2-3)—functions of the hands. Clearly from this passage we learn that our own faithfulness to God is incomplete if thought, passion or action is neglected.

Malachi 2:4-8.

> Know, then, that I have sent this command to you, that my covenant with Levi may hold, says the LORD of hosts. My covenant with him was a covenant of life and well-being, which I gave him; this called for reverence, and he revered me and stood in awe of my name. True instruction was in his mouth, and no wrong was found on his lips. He walked with me in integrity and uprightness, and he turned many from iniquity. For the lips of a priest should guard knowledge, and people should seek instruction from his mouth, for he is the messenger of the LORD of hosts. But you have turned aside from the way; you have caused many to stumble by your instruction.

The last book of the Old Testament, Malachi was written in the fifth century B.C. It is addressed to the people of God after a brutal time in exile, as they had returned to their own land. The central theme of the book is loyalty to God's covenant, a virtue that is particularly evident in Levi the priest. While we sometimes think of God's covenant written on the heart, it is evident here that the covenant involves our minds, affections and actions.

In response to God's covenant, or promise of "life and well-being," Levi responded with reverence and awe, sentiments of the inward self. He evidenced "true instruction" in contrast to the people who had "caused many to stumble by your instruction." Indeed the role of a priest was to "guard knowledge" so that the people "should seek instruction from his mouth." Furthermore he walked with God in "integrity and uprightness" in contrast to the wayward people who had "turned aside from the way." Levi is esteemed as a model because his faith in God incorporated belief with knowledge, which was firmly implanted in his heart and evidenced in his life. One without the other was impossible.

NEW TESTAMENT

John 4:16-18, 21-23.

> Jesus said to her [the Samaritan woman], "Go, call your husband, and come back." The woman answered him, "I have no husband." Jesus said to her, "You are right in saying, 'I have no husband'; for you have had five husbands, and the one you have now is not your husband." . . . Jesus said to her, "Woman, believe me, the hour is coming when you will worship the Father neither on this mountain nor in Jerusalem. You worship what you do not know; we worship what we know, for salvation is from the Jews. But the hour is coming, and is now here, when the true worshipers will worship the Father in spirit and truth."

In his encounter with the Samaritan woman, Jesus overcomes ethnic, religious, gender and moral barriers as he offers her "living water" to satisfy the deepest thirst of the human soul. In the exchange between the two, the topic turns to worship, and Jesus enunciates a perspective on worship that involves the mind, affections and actions. He speaks of worshiping what we know and worshiping in truth, which clearly connotes a cognitive dimension, though the truth element is not limited to the cognitive. Here Jesus is pointing to the object of worship, not the location of worship, which was the focus of the Samaritan people. Moreover, he reminds the woman that true worship will also be in spirit, meaning that our heart must be focused on the object of worship and must engage the deepest recesses of our being.

In his encounter with the Samaritan woman Jesus also implicitly connects worship with moral action. In other New Testament texts, it is made explicit (for example, Rom 12:2; Heb 13:15-16). Jesus invites the woman to call her husband to join in the drinking of the living water. When the woman notes that she has no husband, he points out that, while technically correct, this does not tell the whole story, "for you have had five husbands, and the one you have now is not your husband" (Jn 4:18). The conversation next turns to worship, and it seems clear that Jesus is saying that true worship will entail a pattern of actions that show honor to God. Worship in spirit and truth will incorporate a way of life that reflects the designs and glory of God. Worship that is theologically astute or emotionally alive will not be true worship if one's actions do not correspond. In this encounter Jesus not only accentuates the importance of actions that are congruent with beliefs and affections, but also demonstrates the importance of a proclamation of the good news, which is found in Christ himself.

Romans 1:20-32.

> Ever since the creation of the world his eternal power and divine nature, invisible though they are, have been understood and seen through the things he has made. So they are without excuse; for though they knew God, they did not honor him as God or give thanks to him, but they became futile in their thinking, and their senseless minds were darkened. Claiming to be wise, they became fools; and they exchanged the glory of the immortal God for images resembling a mortal human being or birds or four-footed animals or reptiles.
>
> Therefore God gave them up in the lusts of their hearts to impurity, to the degrading of their bodies among themselves, because they exchanged the truth about God for a lie and worshiped and served the creature rather than the Creator. . . .

For this reason God gave them up to degrading passions. Their women exchanged natural intercourse for unnatural, and in the same way also the men, giving up natural intercourse with women, were consumed with passion for one another. Men committed shameless acts with men and received in their own persons the due penalty for their error.

And since they did not see fit to acknowledge God, God gave them up to a debased mind and to things that should not be done. They were filled with every kind of wickedness, evil, covetousness, malice. Full of envy, murder, strife, deceit, craftiness, they are gossips, slanderers, God-haters, insolent, haughty, boastful, inventors of evil, rebellious toward parents, foolish, faithless, heartless, ruthless. . . . They not only do them but even applaud others who practice them.

If ever there was a passage that brings head, heart and hands together, this is it. It is somewhat typical to read this text as a chronological movement from false thinking, to wayward hearts, to debased moral actions. And while the text moves in that logical order, we see glimpses of the reality that thinking, affections and actions are all integrated together simultaneously. After all, Paul begins this section by stating that "wickedness [sinful actions] suppress[es] the truth" (Rom 1:18).

The language of "understanding," "truth," "thinking" and "knowledge" abounds in this text. Clearly a major part of the depraved way of life, which results in divine judgment, is the mind that has been darkened. Thus false theology has distorted not only truthful accounts of God, but even truthful accounts of the world or nature. Interspersed with this false thinking are hardened hearts, which though recognizing God from his creation, fail to honor God or respond in thanks to the Creator. As a result, God "gave them up in the lusts of their hearts to impurity, to the degrading of their bodies among themselves" (Rom 1:24). This means that God allows their thinking, inner sentiments and outward actions to manifest themselves in their logical and practical consequences.

One manifestation of this is unnatural sexual relations, which is not only a distortion of God's law, but a distortion of nature itself. As one New Testament scholar put it, the "sin of pagans against God comes from their suppression of truth about God in their lives, and as a result their misguided minds have become steeped in idolatry." He goes on to note that God's judgment results "from the moral degradation to which idolatry has brought them: to the craving of their hearts for impurity. Their idolatry has led to moral perversion."[3]

Sometimes we tend to harp on the sins of homosexual lust and action in this passage and fail to note the many actions and character at the end of the chapter. Few of us are exempt from these vices, which include envy, strife, deceit, gossiping, slandering, pride, foolishness and heartlessness.

In reading Romans 1 we often overlook the fact that the vices and actions contrary to God's designs are not only a result of wayward thinking and calloused hearts; these very actions contribute to such thinking and passions. That is, people often change their theology (the head) on sexual matters because of their lifestyle. They want their thinking to be congruent with the way they live, and they want their emotions and will to mesh with their actions. Thus immoral actions frequently lead to distorted understandings. Conversely, moral actions can play a role in helping us see with the mind and be committed with the heart to truthful theological reflection.

The interpenetration of head, heart and hands is particularly evident in sexual matters, because sexual outlook is intimately related to our view of God, creation and humanity. Sexual feelings and actions are powerful forces that are shaped by our cognitive reflections, and in turn those feelings and actions help shape our cognitive reflections about sexuality. Thus right thinking, right affections and right actions are integrated in such a way that when one is missing, the others are affected. We will not get our sexual lives in order unless the head, heart and hands are brought together for the glory of God.

Ephesians 4:17-24.

You must no longer live as the Gentiles live, in the futility of their minds. They are darkened in their understanding, alienated from the life of God because of their ignorance and hardness of heart. They have lost all sensitivity and have abandoned themselves to licentiousness, greedy to practice every kind of impurity. That is not the way you learned Christ! For surely you have heard about him and were taught in him, as truth is in Jesus. You were taught to put away your former way of life, your old self, corrupt and deluded by its lusts, and to be renewed in the spirit of your minds, and to clothe yourselves with the new self, created according to the likeness of God in true righteousness and holiness.

The entire epistle to the Ephesians appeals to thinking, affections and actions. This was particularly necessary for the church in a city that was

the headquarters of the cult of the goddess Diana (or Artemis) whose temple, after being destroyed in the middle of the fourth century BC, had gradually been rebuilt to become one of the seven wonders of the world. Indeed, the success of Paul's mission in Ephesus had so threatened the sale of silver models of her temple that the silversmiths had stirred up a public outcry.[4]

In light of such a context, there was a need to address the mind, the inner self and the outward actions. Thus, in the opening chapter Paul prays that God will "give you a spirit of wisdom and revelation as you come to know him, so that with the eyes of your heart enlightened, you may know what is the hope to which he has called you" (Eph 1:17-18).

In the text from Ephesians 4 above, Paul clearly brings the three elements together. He began by reminding the church that they are no longer to live according to the old patterns, but instead truly to become "God's new society"[5] through grace shown in Jesus Christ. Living the old fallen patterns reflect the "futility of their minds" (v. 17). Paul made a significant appeal to the mind as a vehicle both of sin and of righteousness, for he spoke of darkened understanding, ignorance, teaching, truth in

Christ and the spirit of their minds. But the Ephesian problem was not one of the mind alone, for there was hardness of heart, loss of sensitivity, greed and lust, all of which were to be replaced by a new self in the likeness of God. And the problems of the mind and the heart were intertwined with the way many were living.

In place of the old patterns of unrighteous living, the text calls the Ephesian church and us to a whole new pattern of life (4:25-32) reflecting truth over falsehood, hard work over stealing, management of anger and a forgiveness of others that demonstrates the forgiveness experienced in Christ. Such virtues and actions, however, never emerge in a vacuum and do not spontaneously materialize through God's grace and the power of the Holy Spirit. Rather, they are cultivated through cognitive understanding and commitments to truth, and through a heart that is opened and sensitive to the work of the Holy Spirit within.

1 Timothy 1:3-11.

> Remain in Ephesus so that you may instruct certain people not to teach any different doctrine, and not to occupy themselves with myths and endless genealogies that promote speculations rather than the divine training that is known by faith. But the aim of such instruction is love that comes from a pure heart, a good conscience, and sincere faith. Some people have deviated from these and turned to meaningless talk, desiring to be teachers of the law, without understanding either what they are saying or the things about which they make assertions.
>
> Now we know that the law is good, if one uses it legitimately. This means understanding that the law is laid down not for the innocent but for the lawless and disobedient, for the godless and sinful, for the unholy and profane, for those who kill their father or mother, for murderers, fornicators, sodomites, slave traders, liars, perjurers, and whatever else is contrary to the sound teaching that conforms to the glorious gospel of the blessed God.

This pastoral epistle was written to a young pastor, Timothy, to encourage him in his pastoral work to defend sound doctrine, maintain discipline in the church and remain faithful in his pastoral calling despite vigorous challenges from within. One of the significant challenges that Timothy and other church leaders were facing was false teaching that distorted the core of the gospel and its accompanying theological affirmations. The aim of instruction countering these teachings was not just to engender theological correctness but also "love that comes from a pure heart, a good conscience, and sincere faith" (1 Tim 1:5). Here God's Word is clear that head, heart and hands together must combat forces that would destroy the truth of the gospel and God's Word. No doubt many of us, especially from the evangelical wing of the church, have focused only on the head to defend the gospel and biblical truth.

Love (both the inner virtue and the outward action) does not come by right theology alone, but emerges from a purity of heart, a good conscience and a sincere faith. By the first century B.C. the term *conscience* clearly carried with it the notion that moral principles were known inherently and could be either distorted or enhanced. For the biblical writers, what was known by nature from the heart could be enriched and deepened through the whole person's spiritual development in Jesus Christ. Conscience brings together all elements of the self and plays a crucial role, not only for Christians, but for all human beings who intuitively know the basic contours of God's designs for living. A bad conscience seared by unrighteous and unjust living will distort that intuitive knowledge.

This passage is explicit about the role of actions in Christian life and thought, for the law that describes God's designs for humanity is good when used and understood legitimately. Through the law of God we know what God wants us to do and be and, as seen here, what God does not want us to do and be. But notice that murder, sexual sins, slave trading, lying and so on are not only contrary to God's law. These acts are also "contrary to the sound teaching that conforms to the glorious gospel of the blessed God" (1 Tim 1:10). False actions distort theology, just as false theology distorts actions.

Titus 1:13-16.

> For this reason rebuke them sharply, so that they may become sound in
> the faith, not paying attention to Jewish myths or to commandments of
> those who reject the truth. To the pure all things are pure, but to the cor-
> rupt and unbelieving nothing is pure. Their very minds and consciences
> are corrupted. They profess to know God, but they deny him by their ac-
> tions. They are detestable, disobedient, unfit for any good work.

This epistle was written in part to encourage Titus to teach sound
doctrine in contrast to the false teachers who were influencing the
church. The false teachers were not only distorting the essentials of
Christian theology, but were also actually denying God by their actions,
despite their profession to know God. Their actions were so distorted
that they were "unfit for any good work." All of this is intimately tied to
the fact that "their minds [the head] and their consciences [the heart] are
corrupted."

The epistle does not spell out the false teaching explicitly, but it appears
to be a form of asceticism in which the purity of things like food, marriage,
life in the world and the physical body was being questioned. To dispel
such false thinking the text reminds us that "to the pure all things are pure"
(Tit 1:15). That is, to those whose inner heart and outward actions are in
accordance with God's designs for life, there is a theological correspon-
dence: all things are created by God and are pure (see also 1 Tim 4:1-4).
One of the things we learn from this short text is that heresy (false teaching) in the church can never be handled by theology alone. It is invariably
bound up with the heart and with the hands, for beliefs are intimately connected to who we are inwardly and what we do outwardly.

2 Peter 1:3-11.

> His divine power has given us everything needed for life and godliness,
> through the knowledge of him who called us by his own glory and good-
> ness. Thus he has given us, through these things, his precious and very
> great promises, so that through them you may escape from the corruption

that is in the world because of lust, and may become participants of the divine nature. For this very reason, you must make every effort to support your faith with goodness, and goodness with knowledge, and knowledge with self-control, and self-control with endurance, and endurance with godliness, and godliness with mutual affection, and mutual affection with love. For if these things are yours and are increasing among you, they keep you from being ineffective and unfruitful in the knowledge of our Lord Jesus Christ. . . . Therefore, brothers and sisters, be all the more eager to confirm your call and election, for if you do this, you will never stumble. For in this way, entry into the eternal kingdom of our Lord and Savior Jesus Christ will be richly provided for you.

Peter here is calling us to a godly life that comes "through the knowledge of him who called us by his own glory and goodness" (v. 3). Godly living, as described in this text, is not only about actions but also about inward virtues that come through the knowledge of God. This knowledge of God is not purely cognitive, but is a knowledge of the heart (though the exact language of heart is not used here), which combines both cognitive understanding and deeper understanding from within through the illumination of the Holy Spirit. The virtues espoused are intimately linked together so that one without the other leads to a distortion of godly living. These virtues include goodness, knowledge, self-control, endurance, godliness, mutual affection and love.

The knowledge of God and the virtues that are intertwined with such knowledge lead to a way of life that confirms our calling and assures us of entrance into the eternal kingdom of God. The passage even offers the promise that when such knowledge, inner qualities and outward actions are evident, the believer will "never stumble" (v. 10). This does not imply that we will never struggle or face hardships, but we will, in the overarching pattern of our lives, be able to maintain a growing relationship with Christ. And such growth is dependent on a focus on Christ that incorporates head, heart and hands.

CONCLUSION

Pandita Ramabai made a profound impact on India because she read the Bible through fresh eyes, though in continuity with the classical, apostolic faith. She saw that the Bible brings together the mind, the passions and the actions of presence and proclamation. She understood, as we must understand, that one is not more important than the other. Some of the passages we have explored above start with the mind, others with the heart and still others with action. But all assume an interrelationship of the three. Of course we would not know the role of the heart and hands without the head, but in the realities of everyday life, the three coalesce together in such a way that they are mutually interdependent.

Our minds cannot be brought into harmony with God's designs and truth without hearts that are near to God and actions that reflect God's ways. Our hearts cannot experience the presence and power of the Holy Spirit without knowledge of God to guide us and without actions that reflect the fruit of the Holy Spirit. And our actions of both proclamation and presence will wither without a theology to guide them and a heart to drive and sustain them. Head, heart and hands together. That is the paradigm from God's Word.

DISCUSSION QUESTIONS

1. Deuteronomy 6:1-9 has been a significant passage for making God's law a natural part of life. In our time, how might we make our faith a part of everyday life? What are some contemporary forms of "binding them [commandments] as a sign on your hand . . . writing them on the doorpost of your house"?

2. In Jesus' encounter with the Samaritan woman (Jn 4), how does he bring head, heart and hands together? Jesus refers here to worship in spirit and in truth. What should worship look like when it brings "spirit" and "truth" together? In your experience, are most worship services successful in doing this?

3. In Romans 1:20-32 how do actions influence thinking? How does thinking influence actions? How does the heart relate to thinking and actions in this text? What do you think is the significance of the head-heart-hands paradigm for dealing with the issue of homosexuality in today's culture?

4. Can you think of other biblical passages that bring head, heart and hands together? What do they teach us about the interplay of the three?

9

HEAD, HEART AND
HANDS TOGETHER

An Interdisciplinary Perspective

A few years ago I was speaking on the theme of this book at a conference for pastors. I was attempting to give biblical and theological rationale for head, heart and hands with application to preaching. After one of my sessions, a woman who had spent much of her life in education and was now in ministry commented to me that there was substantial support for my ideas outside the Bible. She noted that a number of psychologists and educational theorists emphasized paradigms that were similar to that of the head, heart and hands. She graciously suggested names and titles, and off to the library I went. I soon discovered that she was right.

While the Bible is the primary source for understanding the integration of thought, passion and action in the Christian life, there is another source to which we can appeal. Many theologians through the centuries speak of a natural theology, which is not void of God as its source, but is known primarily through the natural realm, which is itself God's realm. The doctrine of creation gives theological foundation to this idea, for "if God created the world, it is to be expected that God's creation should bear the mark of the divine handiwork. Just as an artist's distinctive style might be evident in her sculpturing, or a painter might sign his name on his work, so the presence of God . . . can be discerned within the creation."[1]

Understanding the significance of head, heart and hands for Christian thought and life and perceiving their mutual interdependence is evidenced by sources outside the Bible. In particular, scholars from various disciplines, employing reason, observation and empirical research, have arrived at conclusions similar to what the Bible teaches. Namely that the mind, heart and external actions are deeply enmeshed and need each other. There is, of course, a word of caution in all this. Human reason, observation and experiences are not the final arbiter for Christians. All human inquiry is finite and fallen, and often held captive by cultural mores and personal ideologies. Thus we must accept such insights with discernment. They are ultimately secondary to the authority of divine revelation in Christ, the incarnate Word, and the Bible, the written Word.

Nonetheless we can see the significance of head, heart and hands through certain natural enterprises. Moreover, through these disciplines we gain understandings that can enrich our biblical perspectives and help in applying our biblical affirmations. Specifically we will look at three secular disciplines in which at least some thinkers and research have arrived at conclusions about the head, heart and hands that support and enhance the application of biblical teachings on this subject. We will explore the fields of education, social psychology and philosophy.

EDUCATION

Educational theorists have long been interested in how we as humans best learn and the kind of atmosphere needed for such learning. In recent times there has been an increased emphasis in education on the significance of the whole person in the learning process. But this emphasis is not totally new, for two hundred years ago Johann Heinrich Pestalozzi actually used the language of head, heart and hands in his theory of education. On the contemporary scene, Howard Gardner, while not employing the same language, has pointed to holistic learning through what he calls multiple intelligences. Both of these thinkers, and many others could be added, reflect some understandings about the human person that are compatible with the biblical portrayal we have been discussing. Clearly there are also assumptions in their thinking that deviate from a biblical worldview.

Johann Heinrich Pestalozzi. Pestalozzi (1746-1827) was a Swiss social reformer and educator who is widely regarded as being a pioneer of modern childhood education. He advocated education for the poor and emphasized theories of teaching that were designed both to prepare children for life in society and to cultivate their own natural abilities. His pedagogical philosophy stressed a movement from the familiar to the new, the concrete to the abstract, the inclusion of emotion and action as well as reason and the following of a child's natural development.

In many ways Pestalozzi was a child of the Enlightenment, with its emphasis on nature and natural goodness that could be tamed and nurtured through human initiative. While he advocated religious instruction and love as part of the educational process, it is clear that this innovative Swiss thinker deviated from classical Christianity in many of his assumptions about human nature and salvation. As one observer put it, for Pestalozzi "self-perfection was man's religious obligation as well as his moral duty. God through nature had given man his natural moral, intellectual, and physical powers. It was every man's duty to bring these powers to completion."[2]

Nonetheless Pestalozzi had a natural understanding of the human person that was in part congruent with a Christian view of things: namely that we are whole beings, in whom the various parts interface and need to be incorporated into the educational process. He believed that "the aim of all education and instruction is and can be no other than the harmonious development of the powers and faculties of human nature."[3]

What are those powers and faculties of human nature? Pestalozzi writes, "Elementary education is that development and perfecting of the powers and dispositions of the human heart, the human mind, and the human skill which is in accordance with nature." This is what distinguishes humans from animals. In fact Pestalozzi goes on to occasionally use the language of head, heart and hands to describe this human distinctiveness, which comes from the hand of God in nature:

> That alone which takes possession of man as a whole (heart and mind and hand) is educative in the true sense of the word and in accordance with nature; everything which does not take possession of him as a whole does not take possession of him in accordance with nature, and is not, in the true sense of the word, humanly educative.[4]

Pestalozzi was reacting to a hollow form of rationalism, which he perceived to be prominent in his own time and which failed to address the whole person. In contrast he contended for an education that divided itself into three parts corresponding with the head, heart and hands: intellectual education, moral education (through the inner self) and physical education (by which he meant training in physical skills for life in society). He contended, therefore, that education should fit with "the unity of the human faculties [which] was given by God. What, therefore, God hath joined together, let no man put asunder."[5]

For Pestalozzi this meant a radical shift in the structure of schools and instruction and led him to begin several experimental schools. The paradigms and theories were picked up by various thinkers, and today some of his ideas, such as the role of experience in education, have become mainstays. Pestalozzi was insistent, however, that such education did not begin in schools (which needed to be transformed), but rather in the home. "As in elementary education we must consider the education of the heart, the education of the mind, and the education of the body, so the *Book of Mothers* must teach the child, starting from himself as a whole, from his ego, to consider himself, as heart, as mind, and as body." This means that "as body, he is an object for self-perception and feeling; as mind, an object for activity and consciousness of self; as heart, an object for activity of will and sentiment."[6]

Certainly one does not have to buy all of Pestalozzi's educational, moral or religious theories in order to learn from him. What we see most clearly in his thought is something that Christians should clearly affirm for all of education: we are whole beings in whom education must address the head, the heart and the hands. I wonder how different our Christian education institutions and programs would look if we took Pestalozzi seriously. We just might find ourselves being more biblical.

Howard Gardner. Gardner is a professor of cognition and education at Harvard University and an adjunct professor of neurology at Boston University School of Medicine. He is a psychologist who is best known for his concept of multiple intelligences, the notion that there is not just one way of coming to know reality and that the multiple forms of knowing reflect a more holistic approach to education. Gardner is certainly not operating from a Christian perspective and in fact seems to rely heavily on a metaphysic of naturalistic evolution. Nevertheless he makes observations about human nature and learning that can be insightful for a Christian and have a linkage with our head-heart-hands paradigm—though he never uses that language.

Gardner's theory of multiple intelligences challenges the traditional view that intelligence is essentially a singular capacity that can be measured by IQ tests. Drawing from biology, developmental and cognitive psychology, anthropology and neuropsychology, Gardner began to assert that we understand, solve problems and create products in more than one manner. This reflects the fact that as human beings our knowing transcends the sorts of reasoning we typically associate with the mind or cognition.

Gardner has come to speak of eight separate human intelligences. First, there is *linguistic intelligence,* which "involves sensitivity to spoken and written language, the ability to learn languages, and the capacity to use language to accomplish certain goals."[7] Second is *logical-mathematical intelligence,* which performs mathematical operations, investigates scientifically and analyzes logically. These two forms of intelligence are the ones typically valued in educational institutions, and they constitute what many people understand to be intelligence.

The next three intelligences are particularly evident in the arts, but are applied in other ways as well. The third form is *musical intelligence,* which "entails skill in the performance, composition and appreciation of musical patterns." Fourth is *bodily-kinesthetic intelligence,* which involves the utilization of one's whole body or parts of the body to solve problems or fashion products. Dancers, actors and athletes particularly exhibit this form. Fifth, *spatial intelligence* "features the potential to recognize and manipulate the patterns of wide space (those used, for instance, by navigators and pilots) as well as the pattern of more confined areas (such as those of importance to sculptors, surgeons, chess players, graphic artists, or architects)."[8]

There are also in Gardner's research two forms of what he calls personal intelligences. The sixth form is *interpersonal intelligence,* which reflects a person's awareness of other people's feelings, emotions, goals and motivations. This is particularly seen in salespersons, politicians, teachers, counselors and religious leaders. Seventh is *intrapersonal intelligence,* which is the capacity to understand one's own feelings, emotions, capacities and motivations. Gardner's original list included just these above seven, but he has since added one other form, *naturalist intelligence.* By this he means the ability to recognize and classify various objects in one's environment.

Gardner and other researchers have come to believe that "while we all have these eight intelligences, each of us has our own particular blend of them."[9] For education it means that there are varying entry points to tap into a student's intelligence and learning, including such spheres as the narrative, the quantitative, the logical, the aesthetic, the hands-on and the social.

Clearly this theory is not the same as the head-heart-hands paradigm, but it would appear to be somewhat consistent with it. While Gardner's theories and implications taken by some scholars from these theories may not be reflective of Christianity, we find here a framework that reminds us that we do not get at reality in only one way. Even learning, which we commonly associate with the mind, will always utilize diverse processes of the mind and will incorporate dimensions of what I have called the heart and the hands. Unless churches and educational institutions begin to take this seriously, we will go on doing fragmented education, nurturing fragmented lives.

SOCIAL PSYCHOLOGY

Social psychology is an academic discipline that seeks to understand the social behavior of humans. That is, it attempts to understand the relationship between individuals with respect to other social realities, such as groups, institutions or society as a whole. One well-known psychologist, Gordon Allport, defined social psychology as an "attempt to understand and explain how the thought, feeling, and behavior of individuals are influenced by the actual, imagined, or implied presence of others."[10] The attention the discipline gives to thought, feeling and behavior gives it immediate relevance to our theme of head, heart and hands.

In the chapter "Behavior and Attitudes" in a widely used social psychology textbook, David Myers deals explicitly with the relationship of beliefs, feelings and actions, a theme widely researched by social psychologists. Whenever we deal with attitudes, we are tapping into the three dimensions of affect, behavior tendency and cognition. Myers begins his chapter by asking the question, "What is the relationship between what we are (on the inside) and what we do (on the outside)?"[11] The prevailing assumption is that our beliefs and feelings determine our behavior and thus to change behavior (hands) we must change hearts and minds. Myers uses research in social psychology to show that it is not quite so simple.

Past and current research has demonstrated that

> people's expressed attitudes hardly predicted their varying behaviors. Student attitudes toward cheating bore little relation to the likelihood of their actually cheating. Attitudes toward the church were only modestly linked with church attendance on any given Sunday. Self-described racial attitudes provided little clues to behaviors in actual situations.[12]

Take the issue of cheating. In one study, nearly all college students said that it is morally wrong to cheat. However, the researchers had University of Washington students work on an anagram-solving task (which would predict their IQ). They were given instructions that they were to stop working when a bell in the room sounded. When the students were left alone, 71 percent cheated by working past the bell. Interestingly, among the students who worked in front of a mirror and with tape-recorded voices, thus being made self-aware, only 7 percent cheated. That is, expressed attitudes or beliefs alone were not sufficient to impact cheating behavior.

Myers goes on to note that "if social psychology has taught us anything during the last 25 years, it is that we are likely not only to think ourselves into a way of acting but also to act ourselves into a way of thinking."[13] Numerous studies have indicated this, but it is also chronicled in more popular forms, such as actors performing a particular role. Ian Charleson, who played the role of Eric Liddell in the movie *Chariots of Fire,* noted that his whole personality changed as he was playing the role of this very devout, sincere and calm Olympic hero. Action, through the role he played, actually impacted his inner state and self-identity.

The particular social roles people follow have often influenced their explicit behaviors and attitudes. Whether that role is one of student, teacher, soldier or businessperson, we tend to enact behavioral roles that then shape our attitudes, including beliefs and feelings. This can even happen with roles that entail injustices and inhumane treatment. Frederick Douglass was a slave for many years before he became a leader in the abolition movement. He recalls one slave mistress's transformation as she began to act out her new role:

My new mistress proved to be all she appeared when I first met her at the door—a woman of the kindest heart and finest feelings. . . . I was utterly astonished at her goodness. I scarcely knew how to behave toward her. She was entirely unlike any other white woman I have ever seen. . . .

But alas! This kind heart had but a short time to remain such. The fatal poison of irresponsible power was already in her hands, and soon commenced its infernal work. That cheerful eye, under the influence of slavery, soon became red with rage; that voice, made all of sweet accord, changed to one of harsh and horrid discord; and that angelic face gave place to that of a demon.[14]

There are various theories set forth by social psychologists to describe why actions affect attitudes, but for our purposes it is sufficient to simply understand that the relationship of beliefs, feelings and actions is a complex one that defies simplistic explanation. While social psychology research does not discount the role of beliefs in influencing behavior, clearly humans do not act by mind alone. Moreover, our beliefs and our feelings will often be reflective of our actions. Thus, an abundance of research indicates that while most nonsmokers believe that smoking is dangerous to health, significant numbers (at least half in some studies) of smokers disagree with this assertion. When we feel a sense of dissonance between actions and beliefs, we often adjust our beliefs to correspond to our actions.

Unfortunately, in the church we frequently operate from the assumption that our beliefs are purely cognitive and determine our feelings and actions. But as we attempt to understand and minister to people, we will lack wisdom and genuine know-how unless we understand that beliefs are more than cognitive affirmations. Biblical beliefs often do not take root in our lives because we assume that they are simply beliefs, failing to see how the heart and behavior contribute to those beliefs. We will not understand others (or ourselves for that matter) and be fruitful in God's service until we treat people for what they are—a complex matrix of thought, affection and action.

PHILOSOPHY

Traditionally philosophy has been the academic discipline most widely accepted as a vehicle of natural theology. Already in the second and third centuries Christian theologians and apologists were using philosophical reflection to explain and defend the faith. In fact the historic creeds of the church sometimes utilized the language of the philosophers more than the language of the biblical text to articulate certain doctrines. While debates about faith and reason have been vigorous and ongoing, philosophy has sometimes been viewed as the "handmaiden" of theology.

When it comes to understanding human beings as an integration of thought, passion and action, there have been several philosophers who have contributed to this essential paradigm. First, we will look at Thomas Aquinas from the Middle Ages and second, Michael Polanyi from the twentieth century.

Thomas Aquinas. Aquinas (1225-1274) is generally considered to be the greatest philosopher/theologian of the Middle Ages. An Italian who eventually taught at the University of Paris, Aquinas is best remembered for his attempt to synthesize the philosophy of Aristotle with Christian theology.

Aquinas is generally thought of as a Scholastic rationalist. In chapter one we noted that Scholasticism is a classic example of a faith of the head. And while Aquinas does give a certain kind of priority to reason in the order of the human soul, other elements (similar to what we have been calling the heart and the hands) of the soul do influence how we think and act. Clearly knowledge and understanding are the primary and ideal sources of human action and emotions, but Aquinas acknowledges that our actions and affections never purely rest on what we think. Circumstances surrounding our life, our will, our passions and affections, and our inward habits or dispositions all play a role in how we live. For Aquinas the human body, the intellectual dimension, the appetitive dimension and what he called the nutritive dimension are all part of the composite of who we are.

As Aquinas put it, "The will is moved not only by the universal good apprehended by the reason, but also by good apprehended by sense."[15] By *sense* he means the passions of our particular bodily faculties. Passions (which are the same as affections) can certainly go contrary to reason, whereby we are best able to gain a natural grasp of the truth, but passions are not necessarily misleading if they are aimed at the good. Take love as an example. Aquinas said that "since love yearning for the beloved object, is desire; and, having and enjoying it, is joy. Therefore, love is the first of the . . . passions."[16] If our passions, such as love, joy, sadness, hope and fear, are oriented toward the right object, he believes that they can be good and aid even our understanding. However, we can never truly know love unless it is also apprehended or understood through the mind.

We also get some clue as to how Aquinas understood the mind, heart and action in his discussion of habits, which are dispositions toward particular ends. Once again, he begins with the rational mind as the source of our habits, but they do not exist apart from our passions. He puts it this way: "If the will is perverse, these movements, viz., the passions, are perverse also; but if it is upright, they are not only blameless, but even praiseworthy. . . . Therefore moral virtue does not exclude the passions, but is consistent with them." If our passions lead us away from that which is truly good and virtuous or distort true reason, then they must be questioned. "But when it [a passion] follows that judgment, as though being commanded by reason, it helps toward the execution of reason's command."[17] And the execution is always in the body with the body's help, in such a way that our actions, inner dispositions, will and reason cooperate together. Indeed, says Aquinas, "The Philosopher [Aristotle] teaches that habits of virtue and vice are caused by acts."[18]

Though Aquinas is a rationalist, he attends to other dimensions of the human person. Moreover, he allows for the heart dimension and our bodily actions to play a role in understanding and carrying out that understanding, as long as they do not contradict true reason. Thus, in a modified form, Aquinas allows for the interplay of head, heart and hands.

Michael Polanyi. Polanyi (1891-1976) was a world-class chemist who turned to philosophy in midlife out of concern for the way scientific thinking was being used and abused in the world. Polanyi particularly addressed issues in the philosophy of science and epistemology (the branch of philosophy that addresses how we come to know reality). He was born in Budapest to upper-class Jewish parents and, after attaining doctoral degrees in both medicine and physical chemistry, migrated to Berlin and eventually to Manchester University in England.

Polanyi was distressed that the European world was falling apart at the seams through what he believed to be a philosophy of scientific objectivism. For Polanyi the problem was not science or technology per se but a way of thinking about the world that scientific objectivism had engendered. The objectivism of science, on which the modern European world was built, assumed that we could grasp the world with certainty, clarity and without prejudicial value assumptions. Scientific discoveries were totally separated from any human beliefs (such as religion), aspirations or moral commitments. But divorced from a human and moral base, such assumptions were deadly and contributed to the rise of Communism, Nazism and other evils that plundered the thinking and life of modern society, Polanyi concluded.

For Polanyi objectivism was a myth that led to pernicious results. He came to believe, "As human beings, we must inevitably see the universe from a centre lying within ourselves and speak about it in terms of a human language shaped by the exigencies of human intercourse. Any attempt rigorously to eliminate our human perspective from our picture of the world must lead to absurdity."[19] Polanyi was not seeking to do away with the scientific method, which he believed must be utilized in scientific analysis, nor did he capitulate to subjectivism, which is equally disastrous. Rather, he argued that all knowledge has a personal dimension to it, which means that our knowing is more than an activity of the detached, unencumbered mind.

Polanyi argued that many of history's most creative discoveries involved strong personal feelings and commitments. That is, they were not value free, as scientific objectivism contended. He arrived at this conclusion through examining the history of the scientific enterprise, through observation of human deliberation and through his own personal Christian commitment. As to the latter, he appealed to Augustine as an example of a more balanced approach to understanding reality, with his insistence that all knowledge emerges from a stance, a prior commitment. As Augustine had framed it, unless we believe, we do not understand. That is, for a Christian, it is out of one's prior commitment to Christ and the Christian faith (a commitment of heart, soul and mind) that one really comes to understand the theological and moral truths of biblical faith.

Polanyi argued that our beliefs are bound up with our commitments and our predispositions to act in certain ways. Pursuing science without acknowledging one's personal commitments is what makes scientific objectivism so dangerous. It is pawned off as objective truth, free of any personal commitments, when in fact it is laden with all kinds of assumptions and personal commitments. It was this modern objectivism, he contended, which was so hard on religious truth and commitments. "Belief was so thoroughly discredited that . . . modern man lost his capacity to accept any explicit statement as his own belief. All belief was reduced to the status of subjectivity." Polanyi went on to say that, in contrast,

> we must now recognize belief once more as the source of all knowledge. Tacit assent and intellectual passions, the sharing of an idiom and of a cultural heritage, affiliation to a like-minded community: such are the impulses which shape our vision of the nature of things on which we rely for our mastery of things. No intelligence, however critical or original, can operate outside such a fiduciary [trust] framework.[20]

Polanyi referred to this as personal or tacit knowledge, for our understanding always involves the personality and commitments of the one seeking understanding. While he does not utilize the language of head, heart and hands, Polanyi's framework is clearly commensurate with what I have been contending. We experience reality, understand, feel, know and act in ways that bring the total person together.

Polanyi's thought is beginning to make an impact in various corridors of Christianity and in the secular world as well. In his widely heralded *The Structure of Scientific Revolutions,* Thomas Kuhn credits Polanyi with aiding his understanding of the role of paradigm in scientific discovery. Polanyi has particularly garnered interest from people who are trying to steer a middle path between postmodern subjectivism on the one hand and modern objectivism on the other.

I believe that Polanyi's thought can help us in our attempts to articulate, defend and live out the Christian faith. We often feel that we must convince people to buy into Jesus through intellectual arguments, emotive sentiments or Christ-centered actions. Polanyi's paradigm helps us recognize that we can never use only one approach. If people's beliefs are bound up with their prior commitments to act in certain ways, with their deep-seated feelings and with their cognitive reflections, then we will need to present the gospel to the whole person in ways that truly reflect the wholeness of Christ, who brought head, heart and hands together in his own life. Moreover, Christian growth will not come by mere catechism, revival or kingdom-reflecting actions. Only appeals to and experiences of the whole person will enable us to grow and engender spiritual growth in others.

CONCLUSION

In this chapter we have discovered that various disciplines and thinkers support what the Bible teaches: we are whole beings incorporating thought, passion and action. Even secularists, apart from divine revelation, can gain some understanding of the way God has created us.

In some cases, as with Pestalozzi, the actual language of head, heart and hands is utilized. In others the frameworks simply confirm, without explicit use of the language, that our lives can never be dominated by just the mind, the affections (including emotions and will) or human actions. There is an interplay and mutual influence of these three dimensions of our selves. And, as we will see in the final chapter, this interplay makes a huge difference in the way we carry out our Christian calling.

DISCUSSION QUESTIONS

1. What role do you see for natural theology in today's world? What is the biblical basis for natural theology? What role has natural theology played in your own faith?

2. How do you assess Pestalozzi's contention that education should involve the mind, heart and body? What might such education look like in Christian institutions and the church? What are its implications for public education?

3. From reading the sections on social psychology and philosophy, what are the dangers of seeing beliefs as the only or even primary factor in human experience? If beliefs are influenced by behavior, what are the implications for Christian life and thought?

4. What other academic disciplines or fields of thought do you think can make a natural theology contribution to the head-heart-hands paradigm? What insights have you gained from these disciplines or fields?

10

HEAD, HEART AND
HANDS TOGETHER

Implications and Challenges

Recently I had lunch with Craig, one of my former seminary students. I usually hear from such folks when they are facing significant challenges or discouragements, but this young man simply wanted to share with me the good things that were happening in his congregation.

Craig spoke of the depth and vibrancy of their worship services, as they attempted to draw in new forms and maintain some old ones. Life and vitality were replacing the doldrums in worship. He told me about the evening parenting class that he and his wife were running and the significant numbers from the community coming to receive help. From this class, which was meeting a genuine need in the lives of struggling parents, people were also coming to faith in Christ.

Craig shared with me his slow start in preaching in his early years out of seminary, but the sense of growth as he diversified his styles of preaching God's Word. He talked about the enthusiasm people had when they gathered together as fellow believers, the caring for each other and the compassionate spirit that had overflowed into various ministries to meet emotional, economic and health needs in the community. His first few years had been discouraging, causing him to reconsider his call to ministry. Now he was seeing the fruit of his faithfulness and endurance.

As I listened to Craig, it occurred to me that he was experiencing in this church what I was writing about: the growth of head, heart and hands. His church was using its mind to hear God's Word, to discern needs around them and to think strategically of what God wanted them to be doing in their world. The elders and several small groups were even reflecting theologically on what they were doing and why. This church was engaging the heart as their affections, will, emotions and deep-seated understandings reflected a vibrancy, confidence and passion for God. It was evident in their corporate worship and their personal spirituality. And this church was demonstrating a faith of the hands as it engaged in ministries of presence and proclamation. The result was not just numerical growth, but also genuine spiritual growth in love for God and love for neighbor.

If thought, passion and action are significant for the Christian life, it should be evident in the personal and corporate life of believers. But what exactly are the implications for holding them together? What differences should we see in personal and church life if we are attentive to head, heart and hands? And what are the challenges we face in trying to hold them together? These are the themes of this final chapter.

THE IMPLICATIONS

Enriching our mind, inner self and outward actions and allowing them to nurture each other has implications for nearly every phase of life. It will mean that our spirituality isn't just about the heart but about the whole self. It will mean that our theology isn't just a matter of the mind, but will incorporate our passions, what we do and how we do it. It will mean that our marriage and family commitments will bring cognitive understandings, will, emotion, character and actions together. Being a people of the head, heart and hands will mean that evangelism will be done with thoughtfulness, care, excitement and deep dependence on the guidance and empowerment of the Holy Spirit. It will mean that the church's service and social concern ministries will be reflective, active and full of compassion.

But to gain a glimpse of what this all looks like, we will explore four specific areas: worship; evangelism and apologetics; Christian education; and theology, spirituality and Christian practice. What follows are only cursory suggestions, waiting to be fleshed out in our personal and corporate living.

Worship. The current wars over worship are not entirely new. For a long time worship patterns have been divided between those accentuating the mind and those accentuating the heart (particularly its feeling dimension). Today the old divisions, which were once along denominational lines, have now come into the denominations and into individual congregations, and the divisions have become largely focused on specific styles, such as music.

True worship of God should incorporate head, heart and hands. That does not mean that there is just one way to worship or one form that will take precedent over others. Worship, while always rooted in transcendent realities, is very much an act of contextualization. It will look different from one community to the next and one person to the next. But it ought to embody thought, passion and action.

Our worship will be cognitive in that hearing the Word (through Scripture reading and preaching), attention to the lyrics of music, reciting the creeds, prayers and litanies all make use of the mind. In part they also move the mind. Worship without the head will be superficial and tend to tilt off into any direction that emotions or the current mood may lead. Without cognitive reflection, worship will be largely focused on what suits me and my immediate needs.

Without thinking about worship and thinking in worship, we will likely only exacerbate the worship wars. As Marva Dawn has noted, "In this image age in which 'feeling is believing' . . . we often don't ask enough questions or the right kind of questions about the foundations of what we are doing." She goes on to say, "Just as scientists sometimes begin to perform medical procedures before anyone has raised the necessary moral objections, so it seems that many congregations today are switching worship practices without investigating what worship means and how our worship relates to contemporary culture."[1] Some today in the wars over worship have so downplayed the mind that reflection in and about worship is deemed unspiritual. Such attitudes are surely headed to disaster.

Just as worship employs the mind, so it must engage and impact the heart. Jesus put it this way to the Samaritan woman: "God is spirit, and those who worship him must worship in spirit and truth" (Jn 4:24). Our affections and emotions must be deeply involved in true worship of God. Of course we are not all alike emotionally. What moves one person does not move another. Bach will engulf the emotions of some; Delirious? (a British contemporary Christian music group), the emotions of others. But worship that fails to evoke the affective dimension is cutting off a significant portion of our humanness. Emotional response is certainly not the goal of worship, but worship from the deepest recesses of our inner self is essential to worship in truth and spirit.

A significant dimension of heart worship is the practice of the Eucharist, the Lord's Supper. Many believers have viewed this sacrament (or ordinance) as a cognitive ritual in which the bread and the cup are merely symbols that jog our minds back to Calvary. But surely the Lord's Supper is far more than a symbol in the mind. There is in the Eucharist, I believe, a real, mysterious, spiritual presence of Christ, through which he imparts nourishing grace to our lives. It engulfs our total being, including emotions, will and inner sentiments, and has a powerful impact on our spiritual formation.

I recall the day Jan came to see me as her pastor. She was going through debilitating doubts, experiencing one of those "dark nights of the human soul." Jan asked if she should still come to the Lord's Table in the midst of her doubts about Christ, the resurrection, the Bible and divine providence. I replied, "By all means come. You need it now more than ever." Months later with great joy she told me that it was in the mystery of the bread and the wine that her faith was gradually renewed, and Christ again became a living reality in her heart.

And worship ought also to involve the hands. We do not worship primarily as a means toward a certain end, whether that end is evangelism, social action, spirituality or church growth. We worship to glorify God. It is the natural response to the God who created us and redeemed us through Jesus Christ. Its goal is to bring honor that is due the majestic triune God of the universe. Nonetheless worship that is true and vibrant should overflow into everyday actions. When we have encountered God in worship, it is bound to show itself in sharing the good news, living the good news and embodying the justice and mercy of God in a hurting world. It ought to impact the way we work, how we treat a spouse or friends and how we care for the natural world into which its Maker has placed us. An essential element of hearing God's Word in the worship service should be response, and part of response is a commitment to and blessing for moving out of the church and into the world.

I serve on the worship commission at the church in which I am a member. Recently we moved to two services after much prayer, exploration, dialogue and a fair amount of apprehension. One service has a blended style, though still leaning in the direction of traditional forms and music styles. The other is attempting to incorporate more contemporary styles of music, more frequent use of drama, a heavy dose of visual imagery and an informal ethos. Amidst all the anxiety about the two services, the transition is going well and not dividing the congregation.

As I observe what is happening in this smooth transition and exciting venture, it seems to me that the potential divide over styles is being laid to rest because both services are incorporating the full dimensions of the human self, though in different ways. Both services still have a clear appeal to the mind with biblical sermons, the reading of Holy Scripture and some music that appeals to thought and reflection. Both services have an appeal to the heart and emotion through music, litanies and sermons geared that way, though the two services appeal to the heart in different ways. And both services make room for the hands, with opportunities to respond and make commitments that will lead to action. Moreover, there are aesthetic appeals in the setting through banners, symbols and art. There is the use of bodily movement such as occasional dance, silence, multiple forms of prayers, and opportunities for sharing of needs and stories of hope and love. The fear over "worship wars" is subsiding as we move beyond debates about forms and styles to embodying holistic worship of the whole person and the whole body of Christ.

Worship of God has the potential to bring together into a single act the logician, the artist and the activist in ways rarely seen in the rest of society. It has the potential to bring together the logician, artist and activist in each person. We may protest that we are more one than the other, or perhaps none of the three. But worship evokes those gifts and tendencies within each of us and engenders greater experience of them in our lives. It is why worship must be simultaneously rooted deeply in the Word and the reality of God, must be creative in using the full range of our emotional and aesthetic gifts and must be active, as it brings the whole self into an encounter with God that will be evident to the watching world.

Evangelism and apologetics. Evangelism is the telling of the good news of Jesus Christ, through both word and deed, in such a way that hearers have opportunity to respond to God's saving grace. Apologetics is the part of evangelism (though it also serves believers) that responds to the hard questions people inevitably ask about the biblical story and the truth claims of Jesus Christ.

Both evangelism and apologetics have frequently been perceived as acts of the mind. We seek to find the right theology, the best techniques and the most convincing responses to questions in order to demonstrate the validity of the story that Jesus came into the world as the incarnate Son of God, died and rose again to forgive us our sins and bring us into right relationship with God. Apologetics is often defined as a rational attempt to remove the barriers to faith or to find adequate response to questions of doubt, skepticism and hostility. In the modern period, apologetics has had a clear evidentialist and rationalist cast, as it sought to persuade people of the truth of Christianity by thought alone.

Evangelism and apologetics, I suggest, need a new paradigm for our time, and what better than the paradigm of head, heart and hands. Even in their fallen rebellion against God, people seek for God. To appeal only to the mind, or to the affections/emotions, or to human actions is to short-circuit the gospel appeal. It is the whole person that ultimately longs for and needs to encounter the saving work of Jesus Christ. As G. K. Chesterton once quipped, "Every man who knocks on the door of a brothel is looking for God."

Certainly we must appeal to the mind in explaining the meaning of the gospel, in responding to the questions of exploration and doubt and in portraying how the Christian worldview best fits human dreams and aspirations. Though there is much antipathy to reason in our time, humans still ask rational questions that call for thoughtful and relevant answers. The irrationalists of today ironically employ reason to debunk reason. Therefore we need not fear rational thought and must wisely use it.

At the same time evangelism and apologetics need to appeal to the inner sentiments of the heart. As I have noted in earlier chapters, most people who reject Christ do so out of inner reactions, hard experiences or deep-seated struggles. In our postmodern, fragmented age, we need to show how the gospel touches emotion, affections, will and deep-seated understandings. We will need to make use of genre far beyond rational, linear discourse to demonstrate the reality and truthfulness of Jesus Christ. I find it significant that several decades ago the writings of C. S. Lewis that were most effective in evangelism were his rational works like *Mere Christianity* and *Miracles*. Today his most effective writings may be the literary works like the *Chronicles of Narnia, The Great Divorce* and *The Screwtape Letters*. The great genius of Lewis was that this literature professor (note: not theologian) was able to integrate the imaginative and the rational, the right brain and the left.

In speaking to the heart we help people grasp how their will can be transformed into doing not what comes easy, but what we know we ought to do and God wants us to do. Appealing to the heart enables our contemporaries to experience how our good but fallen emotions can be transformed by God's power, so that we are no longer captive to them but employ them with balance and care. Addressing the heart speaks to the deepest human aspirations and affections, so that humans can begin to see the way Christ meets, challenges and empowers those aspirations and affections. Alan Jacobs of Wheaton College suggests that one of the tasks of contemporary apologetics "is to argue that Christianity can tell a better story—that is, a more coherent narrative, one that accounts more accurately and completely for the events of our lives, one that can give our lives meaningful direction—a better story, then, than any of its rivals."[2] Such is an appeal not only to the mind but also to the heart.

Evangelism and apologetics also need to appeal to the hands. In the early church, one of the strongest evidences employed by the apologists in defending Christianity against the civil and philosophical challenges was the character and actions of the church itself. The proof was in the pudding. In the earliest days of Christianity there was evidence that

> Christians had constituted a new kind of community, one that was independent of the social and political institutions of the Roman Empire; it was not territorial, i.e., defined by people or region or city, and its central rite, the Sacrifice, as it was called in Christian antiquity, embraced old and young, male and female, slave and free, gentile and Jew, rich and poor, educated and uneducated. Such a community was without precedent, and it figured large in the theological response to pagan criticism of Christianity.[3]

The character and quality of our lives, individually and collectively as the church, is perhaps the most convincing argument for the truth of

Christ. This does not mean that truth is determined by pragmatism (that is, what works), but it does mean that humans want evidence in real life for deciding what they will ultimately give themselves to. When nonbelievers see our truth claims and our worldviews lived out in the push and pull of social and personal struggles, see a compelling rendition of the Christ we confess, and see a community of love and compassion rooted in truth, they will have experienced the most effective evangelism.

One InterVarsity chapter did a Habitat for Humanity project with the gay/lesbian group on their campus. Of course they differed on many things, but they did agree that people need homes, and thus they worked together and built relationships. This concrete example of faith in action, breaking down walls of hostility, was no doubt even more powerful than rational arguments about the truthfulness of the Christian gospel and the Christian ethic.

Down through the ages the challenges of pain and suffering, the fate of unbelievers, the questions of supernaturalism and the validity of the historical narratives surrounding Christ's death and resurrection have always been present. The secular, pluralistic, spiritualistic orientation of our own time simply gives new nuances to old questions. Responses to these challenges will employ the mind and appeal to the heart, but they must always embody actions that reflect a new reality in the lives of believers. Thus a community that cares deeply for people in the midst of pain and suffering reinforces our philosophical musings about pain and suffering. A community that lives out the transcendent truth of the risen Christ demonstrates and emboldens the reality that on the third day a man who was dead rose from the grave. In this sense we can come to "understand the church itself—a visible, corporate expression of the Christian worldview—to be an apologetic."[4]

Christian education. Christian education is the ongoing task of the Christian community to equip believers for living out the ways of Christ and God's Word with reference to the contexts in which they find themselves. Christian education will run the gamut from traditional Sunday school classes, to small-group Bible studies, to Christian primary and secondary schools, to Christian colleges and universities, to theological seminaries. All seek a common end in different ways and at different levels.

Education is commonly understood as a cognitive enterprise. Through critical inquiry we seek to enable an understanding of the physical and biological world, history, mathematics, social and personal life, specialized forms of applied knowledge and many other spheres of human existence. In Christian education we additionally seek to understand the Bible, theology, church traditions, forms of spirituality and worship, as well as the contours and challenges of contemporary culture. We seek also to bring our biblical and theological understandings into engagement with the traditional academic disciplines. In all of this, education of the mind and with the mind is essential. We must engage the whole world with the wonderful gift of thinking that God has given to us.

But as we noted in the last chapter, educational philosophy and research has demonstrated that we do not learn by mind alone. Our deepest affections and our emotional states have a significant bearing on what we will open our minds to and on how we actually process knowledge. And of course we all know what research demonstrates: we learn by doing. As Parker Palmer has written, "To teach is to create a space where the community of truth is practiced."[5]

Contemporary Christian education, in all its phases and at all levels, needs to give attention to holistic learning. Learning with the mind alone will be lifeless, deemed irrelevant and have little sustaining power in either recall or application. At the same time the whole mind in all its styles of learning needs to be employed so that our thinking and action is not moved merely by emotions. A people that believe in truth will not succumb to the postmodern tendency of denigrating thought (including reason) and reflection.

But we must remind ourselves that truth is not merely a cognitive reality. Truth is that which is real, and we will best encounter the real about

God, self and the world through an educational process that brings together intellectual inquiry, sentiments of our inward selves and the actions of the human body. When all three are oriented toward God, the ultimate Truth and Source of all knowledge, we have the best shot at really knowing truth that is essential for being the kind of people God desires. It will then be a knowledge that permeates every fiber of our being and hence is more easily transferable to those we teach, nurture or lead by example.

Many educational institutions are finding that "contextual education" affords the best opportunity for holistic education. Internships, service learning and international studies all have the potential to engage the whole person in ways that incorporate thought, passion and action. I am personally aware of several institutions that have employed head, heart and hand categories (though perhaps using other language) to establish goals and mechanisms for evaluation. During my time at Messiah College, we established the mission and specific goals of our College Ministries programs under the three rubrics, and it gave us very clear criteria for evaluating our programs. Each of the twenty goals we established were classified as either head, heart or hands goals, with a clear aim of engaging the whole person. Such can easily be adapted for any kind of educational program.

Theology, spirituality and Christian practice. It is quite common to separate theology, spirituality and Christian practices (such as moral actions) into three separate domains. The common portrayal is that theology (with the mind) is the foundational core from which emerges spirituality and action. This often leads to a perceived disconnection between theology and everyday "real" life. The distinction between "theoretical sciences" and "practical sciences" goes back to Aristotle, who contended that the aim of theoretical science is truth, while the aim of practical science is human action. In such a rendition, theology is often deemed the foundational and salient partner, with spirituality (the heart) and human practices or action (the hands) flowing from the mind.

Such a paradigm, however, owes more to Western philosophy than it does to the Bible. We saw in the previous two chapters that both special revelation and natural revelation portray head, heart and hands in an interactive, mutually influencing pattern. As theologian Dorothy Bass notes, "There is an integral relationship between how we live and what we can know of God, other people and the world. What we believe is entangled with what we do. We can believe more fully as we act more boldly. And we can act more boldly as we believe more fully."[6] And we should add, I believe, that we believe and act more fully as our heart is more fully engaged with God.

Bass, Miroslav Volf and a number of other theologians have contended that one way to think about all this is through the concept of Christian practices, which in everyday life embody our beliefs and sentiments and simultaneously help shape those beliefs. Volf, a native of the former Yugoslavia and now teaching at Yale Divinity School, tells the story of a rather rough, uncouth guest who would often come to his father's small Pentecostal church for Communion and the Sunday meal that followed. As a young boy, Volf often felt uncomfortable with the man's unkempt style and manners, but his parents repeatedly invited the man back. Volf writes, "In their own minds . . . they were extending the invitation to this stranger because they did not think one should hold the table of the Lord at which my father presided in the morning apart from the table of our home at whose head he was sitting at noon." Had Volf objected to the man's presence they would have responded, "As the Lord gave his body and blood for us sinners, so we ought to be ready to share not only our belongings, but also something of our very selves with strangers."

Volf goes on to note, "The circle of our table was opened up by the wounds of Christ, and a stranger was let in. Had I continued to protest, they would have reminded me of that grand eschatological meal whose host will be the Triune God, a meal at which people of every tribe and tongue will be feasting. I had better be ready to sit next to him at that meal."[7] Volf contends that good theology needs not only a compelling intellectual vision, but also a compelling way of life.

All of this does not mean that our theology merely arises out of human actions or "praxis," as some renditions of liberation theology have contended. Volf notes, "We engage in practices for the sake of God: we don't construe a picture of God so as to justify engagement with a particular set of practices. . . . Adequate beliefs about God cannot be ultimately grounded in a way of life; a way of life must be grounded in adequate beliefs about God."[8] But the practice of our faith will go a long way in making our beliefs about God and Christian theology more compelling and relevant to everyday life. And these practices themselves are part and parcel of Christian truth.

Thus, theology, spirituality and Christian practice can never be separated. Our beliefs, inner sentiments and actions are all part of each other. We will have a greater chance of getting our theology right if our affections and actions are in accordance with the truth of the living God and God's revealed patterns. We will have a greater chance of being drawn closer to the intimate presence and power of God if our thinking and practices accord with God's designs. And we will have a greater chance of getting our actions and practices right when our minds and hearts are rooted in and captured by the reality of the living, triune God.

In the life of the church and in Christian education we will no doubt separate out theology, spirituality and ethics for the sake of pedagogical understandings. But they need each other and will be enriched by each other, and every believer and church needs always to embody head, heart and hands.

THE CHALLENGES

Most of us find it quite difficult to hold head, heart and hands together. As Robert Mulholland, a seminary professor, wrote, "Left to ourselves in the development of our spiritual practices, we will generally gravitate to those spiritual activities that nurture our preferred pattern of being and doing. The shadow side of our preference pattern will languish unattended and unnurtured."[9] Thus some of us will focus primarily on the mind as the key to the Christian life, others of us will focus on the heart, and still others will focus on the hands. Why? There seem to be several interacting factors that set us in these directions, including our cultures, church backgrounds and personalities.

Cultures. Cultures provide us with our most fundamental patterns of outlooks, beliefs, attitudes, feelings and actions. Culture is a kind of mental map that our society passes on to guide us in everyday life. Cultures are by no means deterministic in the sense of uniformly determining certain patterns and tendencies, for individuals bring their own unique personalities and choices into interaction with cultural expectations. Nonetheless cultures have a powerful impact on our perspectives, ways of being and patterns of doing. And cultures often predispose us in directions of the head, heart or hands, though a given culture is never purely one or another.

Anthropologist Ruth Benedict once described cultures as tending to be primarily either Apollonian or Dionysian, picking up on the descriptions of Greek tragedies as discussed by the philosopher Nietzsche. Dionysian cultures are those in which people tend to break ordinary limits of existence and express themselves with strong emotion and ecstasy. The Dionysian "seeks to attain in his most valued moments escape from the boundaries imposed on him by his five senses, to break through into another order of experience. The desire of the Dionysian, in personal experience or in ritual, is to press through it toward a certain psychological state, to achieve excess."[10] In short, Dionysian cultures tend to be oriented toward the heart.

In contrast, Apollonian cultures distrust the excessive and emotional. The Apollonian "keeps the middle of the road, stays within the known map, does not meddle with disruptive psychological states. . . . The known map, the middle of the road, to any Apollonian is embodied in the common tradition of his people."[11] These cultures are inclined to be a people of the head with their appeal to measured reason, balance and tradition.

One must always be careful in cultural analysis lest we fall prey to stereotypes and oversimplification. But clearly some of us come from cultural backgrounds that have predisposed us to a strong cognitive orientation. Others of us are from cultures that have socialized us to look within to our feelings, desires and affections in making decisions and carrying out our lives. Still others of us are from cultures that prize action and doing as the heart of being responsible or mature human beings. These cultural backgrounds clearly incline us toward one type in our own Christian experience and expression.

Church backgrounds. Closely related to cultures are church backgrounds, which have socialized us into a particular expression of Christian faith. In a sense these traditions are kinds of subsocieties with their own subcultural expectations. Here too we must be careful not to oversimplify and stereotype given denominations or individual churches.

But as we saw in the first chapter, there are church traditions and parachurch movements that have a propensity toward one type over the others. Some of us come from creedal traditions in which understandings of the creeds are perceived to be the most salient feature in shaping Christian experience. Similarly, some of us come from noncreedal churches that are nonetheless head oriented with their strong emphasis on the centrality of biblical and theological knowledge as the key to Christian life and maturity. If we are socialized in those churches, we will likely prize a Christian mind above all else.

Others of us come from church backgrounds that value emotion, affections, desire and deep-seated inner understandings as the key to the spiritual life. For these traditions the heart is both the means to Christian vitality and the criterion through which we judge authentic faith. If we are socialized in these churches we will likely view the faith through the lens of our inward selves and seek to know God primarily through affections and emotions.

Still others of us come from church backgrounds that accentuate human actions, whether that be proclamation (evangelism) or presence (social concern and service). For these traditions the hands are the means of growing in Christ and the evidence that our faith is valid. If we are socialized in these churches we will likely view the faith as primarily a set of actions reflecting Christ.

In a post-denominational world in which people no longer choose individual churches primarily on the basis of denomination, we may feel that church backgrounds are no longer significant in shaping our faith expression. But the reality is that all believers are shaped by some tradition, be it denominational, congregational or parachurch. And each of these traditions has a tendency to predispose us toward head, heart or hands.

Personalities. Though cultures and church backgrounds play a significant role in our orientation to faith, these factors always interface with our unique personalities. Psychologists have long debated what exactly forms our personalities, but the shape of a personality is certainly more than the accumulation of family, church and societal backgrounds. The personality debates generally focus on the roles of nature (what we inherit biologically) versus nurture (the way we were socialized). When it comes to our faith orientations, personality is a factor in whether we are focused primarily on thought, passion or action.

One way of reflecting on all this is through the famous Myers-Briggs personality profile, based on the thinking and research of Swiss psychoanalyst Carl Jung. This is not the place to go into detail on this widely used personality indicator, but the categories and profiles clearly have implications for the head-heart-hands paradigm. Mulholland has utilized the Myers-Briggs personality categories to think about spiritual formation and the ways in which our personalities influence our spiritual journey. For example, "extroverts will tend to develop a highly social spirituality which involves them in spiritual activities with others, but avoid the solitude and reflection that would bring depth and perspective to their life and others."[12] That is, extroverts often end up with a faith of the hands.

One aspect of the profile looks at thinking versus feeling orientations in making choices. Mulholland notes that thinking personalities tend to be more theological and analytical in their spirituality: "Should thinking be one of our preferences, we will tend to be cerebral in our spirituality. We will appreciate reason as the means through which we encounter God; we'll tend to be analytical and theoretical in our wrestling with the Scripture." We will likely be more a person of the head. On the other hand, if feeling is our preference, "our spiritual habits will tend to focus more on relationships—with God and others. We will encounter God through our relationship and the emotions attendant on them."[13] We will likely be a person of the heart.

Of course we could go into much more detail in all this, including the various personality configurations and their relationship to the head-heart-hands framework. My point is simply that a significant part of our orientation will be a result of our personalities, and our personality orientation sometimes makes it difficult to hold thought, passion and action together in harmony.

CONCLUSION

Because of the influence of culture, backgrounds and personality, it is often a challenge to bring head, heart and hands together in a joyous symphony. We tend to feel safe with the familiar style and orientation that we have long known. In dealing with this predicament we must be careful not to negate our cultures, backgrounds or personalities, for each are gifts of God in shaping our selves. Moreover, God often uses our natural propensities in carrying out his work through us in the world.

At the same time, all cultures, backgrounds and personalities are finite and fallen. Redemption in Christ does not obliterate or completely overturn them, but rather begins a transformational process that brings them into greater harmony with God's designs. While we will likely always have a tendency toward the head, the heart or the hands, growth in Christ can overcome the divide and engender within us a greater harmony be-

tween the three. Each of us as individuals and as collective bodies seems
to have default settings in one of the three directions. But God's grace and
power is at work transforming us within our own default settings.

God desires that we become whole beings who learn to experience
God and his ways though the gifts of the mind, affections and actions. It
is in the mutual interdependence of head, heart and hands that we come
to a fuller realization of God's creation and redemptive purposes through
grace and the power of the Holy Spirit. While here on earth, we begin
the transformation of our total selves into that greater reality which
awaits us in heaven, when mind, affections and body will reflect completely the glory and grandeur of the triune God. And the transforming
process now must always transpire in the context of the Christian community, where we have the best shot of experiencing all of the gifts and
resources God has for us.

But holding head, heart and hands together in unity is important not
only for our personal lives or even the life of the church. In a fragmented,
postmodern world that frequently lacks cohesion and meaning, this paradigm holds out the greatest possibility for God using us in his world.
The bringing together of reason, emotion, human experience and
action—all under the lordship of Christ—has the potential of making a
significant impact on our world for the glory of God.

The modern world (eighteenth through twentieth centuries) aimed
at unity, but through specialization tended to separate human thinking,
feeling and acting. In the church it separated theology from spirituality,
action from thought, evangelism from social justice and God from the
details of everyday life. In the postmodern world the separations continue, as we experience reality in fragmented ways, making wholeness
of life a difficult achievement. But underneath all the separations, frag-
mentations and skepticisms of our time, there is a human longing—a
longing for ultimacy, true selfhood, unity with others, integration of
personal life and authentic actions that reflect who we really are and
what we really believe.

A Christian faith of the head, heart and hands holds forth the best option for meeting these deep longings in our age. Bringing our minds, deepest passions and actions together into a harmonious whole with Christ at the center has the potential to be a powerful witness to a world that has lost its way amid the cacophony of voices and laments in our time. The joyous consort stands apart from any other compelling paradigm—whether it be from pop psychology, fad spiritualities, traditional religions or academic disciplines—in pointing the way to truth, humanness, mercy, justice, wholeness and divine restoration. It comes through the One who in the incarnation embodied all that we are meant to be and now calls us to love the Lord our God with head, heart and hands.

DISCUSSION QUESTIONS

1. Why is an evangelism/apologetics approach that appeals to head, heart and hands more adequate than an appeal to the mind or emotions alone? Have you observed apologetic or evangelism efforts that bring the three together? Beyond the suggestions made in this chapter, what other appeals of the head, heart and hands do you think would be appropriate in defending Christianity in our postmodern world?

2. Why is it important to bring theology, spirituality and Christian practice together? What are some Christian practices that illuminate and reinforce particular Christian beliefs?

3. As you think about your own expression of faith in terms of head, heart and hands, which of the three factors (culture, church background, personality) have most influenced you? What other factors do you think have shaped your faith orientation?

4. As you think to the future, how do you hope to blend head, heart and hands? What concrete steps can you take to keep them together and allow them to enrich each other for the glory of God?

NOTES

Preface

[1] I have written two articles focusing on the theme of this book: "The Three Hs of Christian Maturity," *Reformed Journal* 37, no. 1 (1987): 12-16; and "Living the Truth: A Faith of the Head, Heart, and Hands," *C. S. Lewis Institute Report*, Fall 2000, pp. 3-4, 9-10.

Chapter 1: Fragmented Faith and Fragmented People

[1] J. P. Moreland, *Love Your God with All Your Mind: The Role of Reason in the Life of the Soul* (Colorado Springs: NavPress, 1997), pp. 65, 67.

[2] Alister McGrath, *Christian Theology: An Introduction*, 2nd ed. (Oxford: Blackwell, 1997), p. 34.

[3] Richard A. Muller, *God, Creation and Providence in the Thought of Jacob Arminius* (Grand Rapids: Baker, 1991), p. 32.

[4] Roger Olson, *The Story of Christian Theology: Twenty Centuries of Tradition and Reform* (Downers Grove, Ill.: InterVarsity Press, 1999), p. 476.

[5] Charles Hodge, *Systematic Theology*, 3 vols. (New York: Scribners, 1899), 1:10.

[6] McGrath, *Christian Theology*, p. 221.

[7] Barry Callen, *Authentic Spirituality: Moving Beyond Mere Religion* (Grand Rapids: Baker, 2001), p. 18.

[8] Quoted in Karen Armstrong, *Visions of God: Four Medieval Mystics and Their Writings* (New York: Bantam, 1994), p. 175.

[9] Ibid., p. 73.

[10] Olson, *Story of Christian Theology*, p. 477.

[11] Johann Arndt, *True Christianity*, in *Pietism*, Christian Classics, ed. Thomas Halbrooks (Nashville: Broadman, 1981), p. 165.

[12] Richard Foster, *Streams of Living Water: Celebrating the Great Traditions of Christian Faith* (San Francisco: HarperSanFrancisco, 1998), p. 99.

[13] Both are quoted in Donald Bloesch, *The Holy Spirit: Works and Gifts* (Downers Grove, Ill.: InterVarsity Press, 2000), pp. 193, 195.

[14] Roger Robbins, "Pentecostal Movement," in *The Dictionary of Christianity in America*, ed. Daniel Reid et al. (Downers Grove, Ill.: InterVarsity Press, 1990), p. 887.

[15] Foster, *Streams of Living Water*, p. 199.

[16] Dwight L. Moody, *New Sermons* (New York: Goodspeed, 1880), p. 535.

[17]Walter Rauschenbusch, *Christianizing the Social Order* (New York: Macmillan, 1912), p. 125.
[18]Robert Handy, "The Social Gospel Movement," in *Dictionary of Christianity in America,* ed. Daniel Reid et al. (Downers Grove, Ill.: InterVarsity Press, 1990), p. 1105.
[19]Gustavo Gutiérrez, *A Theology of Liberation* (Maryknoll, N.Y.: Orbis, 1973), p. 88.

Chapter 2: Christian Faith and the Head

[1]Mark A. Noll, *The Scandal of the Evangelical Mind* (Grand Rapids: Eerdmans, 1994), p. 3.
[2]Aristotle, "Metaphysics," 1.1 in *The Complete Works of Aristotle,* vol. 2, ed. Jonathon Barnes (Princeton: Princeton University Press, 1984), p. 1552.
[3]Quoted in John Stott, *Your Mind Matters* (Downers Grove, Ill.: InterVarsity Press, 1972), p. 19.
[4]James Orr, *The Christian View of God and the World as Centering in the Incarnation* (Edinburgh: Andrew Eliot, 1893), p. 4.
[5]David Naugle, *Worldview: The History of a Concept* (Grand Rapids: Eerdmans, 2002), p. xvii.
[6]Francis Fukuyama, *Our Posthuman Future: Consequences of the Biotechnology Revolution* (New York: Farrar, Straus & Giroux, 2002), p. 14.

Chapter 3: Distortions of the Head

[1]Mark A. Noll, *The Scandal of the Evangelical Mind* (Grand Rapids: Eerdmans, 1994), pp. 46, 47.
[2]Rodney Stark, *For the Glory of God: How Monotheism Led to Reformations, Science, Witch-Hunts, and the End of Slavery* (Princeton, N.J.: Princeton University Press, 2003), p. 53.
[3]Augustine, "Teaching Christianity," *De Doctrina Christiana* in *The Works of St. Augustine: A Translation for the Twenty-first Century* (Hyde Park, N.Y.: New City Press, 1996), 2:159-60.
[4]Rudolf Otto, *The Idea of the Holy* (New York: Oxford University Press, 1923), p. 3.
[5]Quoted in Philip Yancey, *Finding God in Unexpected Places* (Ann Arbor, Mich.: Servant, 1997), pp. 107-8.
[6]W. Jay Wood, *Epistemology: Becoming Intellectually Virtuous* (Downers Grove, Ill.: InterVarsity Press, 1998), pp. 34-40. See also the extended listing of these virtues in James Sire, *Habits of the Mind: Intellectual Life as a Christian Calling* (Downers Grove, Ill.: InterVarsity Press, 2000), p. 109.
[7]John Henry Newman, *The Idea of a University,* ed. Frank M. Turner (New Haven, Conn.: Yale University Press, 1996), p. 45.

Chapter 4: Christian Faith and the Heart

[1]Agnieszka Tennant, "Ragamuffin: The Patched-Up Life and Unshabby Message of Brennan Manning," *Christianity Today,* June 2004, p. 42.
[2]Brennan Manning, *Abba's Child: The Cry of the Heart for Intimate Belonging* (Colorado Springs: NavPress, 1994), p. 22.
[3]Blaise Pascal *Pensees* 4.277.
[4]Mark A. McIntosh, *Mystical Theology: The Integrity of Spirituality and Theology* (Malden, Mass.: Blackwell, 1998), p. 5.
[5]Dallas Willard, *Renovation of the Heart: Putting on the Character of Christ* (Colorado Springs:

NavPress, 2002), p. 142.

[6]Jonathan Edwards, *Religious Affections,* ed. John E. Smith (New Haven, Conn.: Yale University Press, 1959), p. 95.

[7]Ibid., pp. 97, 98.

[8]Antonio Damasio, *Looking for Spinoza: Joy, Sorrow and the Feeling Brain* (Orlando: Harcourt, 2003), p. 28.

[9]Willard, *Renovation of the Heart,* p. 117.

[10]C. S. Lewis, *The Magician's Nephew* (New York: Macmillan, Collier, 1970), p. 125.

[11]Quoted in Brad Walton, *Jonathan Edwards, Religious Affection and the Puritan Analysis of True Piety, Spiritual Sensation and Heart Religion* (Lewiston, N.Y.: Edwin Mellen Press, 2002), pp. 156-57.

[12]Willard, *Renovation of the Heart,* p. 19.

[13]Manning, *Abba's Child,* p. 21.

Chapter 5: Distortions of the Heart

[1]Quoted in Barry Callen, *Authentic Spirituality: Moving Beyond Mere Religion* (Grand Rapids: Baker, 2001), p. 18.

[2]Richard J. Foster, *Prayer: Finding the Heart's True Home* (San Francisco: Harper, 1992), p. 1.

[3]Diogenes Allen, "Intellectual Inquiry and Spiritual Formation," in *Inquiring After God: Classic and Contemporary Readings,* ed. Ellen T. Charry (Oxford: Blackwell, 2000), p. 19.

[4]David Naugle, *Worldview: The History of a Concept* (Grand Rapids: Eerdmans, 2002), p. 260.

[5]Quoted in James Sire, *Habits of the Mind: Intellectual Life as a Christian Calling* (Downers Grove, Ill.: InterVarsity Press, 2000), p. 82.

[6]Thomas Kelly, *A Testament of Devotion* (New York: Harper & Row, 1941), p. 29.

[7]For a helpful overview of contemporary trends in spirituality see Robert Wuthnow, *After Heaven: Spirituality in American Since the 1950s* (Berkley: University of California Press, 1998).

[8]See Whitney Cross, *The Burned-Over District: The Social and Intellectual History of Enthusiastic Religion in Western New York, 1800-1850* (Ithaca, N.Y.: Cornell University Press, 1950).

[9]Richard Foster, *Celebration of Discipline: The Path to Spiritual Growth* (New York: Harper & Row, 1978), p. 1.

Chapter 6: Christian Faith and the Hands

[1]Dallas Willard, *Renovation of the Heart: Putting on the Character of Christ* (Colorado Springs: NavPress, 2002), p. 161.

[2]In many countries, abortion has been granted not by the judicial system but by laws passed in their highest legislative body.

[3]This is a summary of the World Council of Churches document from some years ago in David J. Bosch, *Witness to the World: The Christian Mission in Theological Perspective* (Atlanta: John Knox Press, 1980), p. 36.

[4]Arthur P. Johnston, *The Battle for World Evangelism* (Wheaton: Tyndale House, 1978), p. 18.

[5]John Stott, *Christian Mission in the Modern World* (Downers Grove, Ill.: InterVarsity Press, 1975), p. 30.

[6]Ronald J. Sider, *Genuine Christianity: Essentials for Living Your Faith* (Grand Rapids: Zonder-

van, 1996), p. 11.

[7]Lesslie Newbigin, *The Gospel in a Pluralist Society* (Grand Rapids: Eerdmans, 1989), p. 125.

[8]Quoted in Stott, *Christian Mission,* p. 108.

[9]For a detailed treatment of ethics, I suggest my own book *Choosing the Good: Christian Ethics in a Complex World* (Grand Rapids: Baker Academic, 2002).

[10]International Justice Mission, <http://www.ijm.org/ijm_at_work.html>. (Accessed on September 10, 2004.) See also Gary Haugen, *Good News About Injustice: A Witness of Courage in a Hurting World* (Downers Grove, Ill.: InterVarsity Press, 1999).

[11]Sider, *Genuine Christianity,* p. 14.

Chapter 7: Distortions of the Hands

[1]Stanley Hauerwas, *With the Grain of the Universe: The Church's Witness and Natural Theology* (Grand Rapids: Brazos, 2001), p. 215.

[2]Ellen T. Charry, ed., *Inquiring After God: Classic and Contemporary Readings* (Oxford: Blackwell, 2000), p. xviii.

[3]Charles Grandison Finney, *Lectures on Revivals of Religion,* ed. William G. McLoughlin (Cambridge, Mass.: Harvard University Press, 1960), pp. 287-88.

[4]Os Guinness, *Dining with the Devil: The Megachurch Movement Flirts with Modernity* (Grand Rapids: Baker, 1993), p. 38.

[5]In making this point I am not implying that there are no biblical grounds for divorce. I believe that there are legitimate divorces on biblical and theological grounds, but I also believe that many divorces today are out of self-centeredness, which is not a sufficient ground for dissolving a marriage. The moral presumption is always on the side of maintaining our marriage covenants.

[6]Noted in David J. Bosch, *A Spirituality of the Road* (Scottdale, Penn.: Herald, 1979), p. 71.

[7]N. T. Wright, *For All God's Worth: True Worship and the Calling of the Church* (Grand Rapids: Eerdmans, 1997), p. 101.

Chapter 8: Head, Heart and Hands Together: The Biblical Case

[1]Ramabai Sarasvati and Meera Kosambi, *Pandita Ramabai Through Her Own Words: Selected Works* (Oxford: Oxford University Press, 2000), as quoted in <http://www.born-again-christian.info/pandita.ramabai.biography.htm> (accessed on September 17, 2004).

[2]William LaSor, David Hubbard and Frederic Bush, *Old Testament Survey: The Message, Form and Background of the Old Testament* (Grand Rapids: Eerdmans, 1982), p. 181.

[3]Joseph Fitzmyer, S.J., *Romans: A New Translation with Introduction and Commentary* (New York: Doubleday, 1993), p. 271.

[4]John R. W. Stott, *The Message of Ephesians: God's New Society* (Downers Grove, Ill.: InterVarsity Press, 1979), p. 23.

[5]Ibid., pp. 24-27.

Chapter 9: Head, Heart and Hands Together: An Interdisciplinary Perspective

[1]Alister McGrath, *Christian Theology: An Introduction,* 2nd ed. (Oxford: Blackwell, 1997), p. 187.

[2]Gerald Lee Gutek, *Pestalozzi and Education* (New York: Random House, 1968), p. 65.
[3]Quoted in A. Pinloche, *Pestalozzi and the Foundation of the Modern Elementary School* (New York: Charles Scribner's Sons, 1901), p. 125.
[4]Ibid., p. 165.
[5]Ibid., p. 166.
[6]Ibid., p. 211.
[7]Howard Gardner, *Intelligence Reframed: Multiple Intelligences for the 21st Century* (New York: BasicBooks, 1999), p. 41.
[8]Ibid., p. 42.
[9]Project Sumit, "Theory of Multiple Intelligences," <www.pz.harvard.edu/sumit/misumit.htm> (accessed on April 20, 2004).
[10]Quoted in Morris Rosenberg and Ralph Turner, eds., *Social Psychology: Sociological Perspective* (New Brunswick: Transaction Publishers, 1990), p. ix.
[11]David Myers, *Social Psychology*, 7th ed. (New York: McGraw Hill, 2002), p. 131.
[12]Ibid.
[13]Ibid., p. 136.
[14]Quoted in ibid., p. 139.
[15]Thomas Aquinas *Summa Theologica* 1-2.10.3.
[16]Ibid. 1-2.25.2.
[17]Ibid. 1-2.59.3.
[18]Ibid. 1-2.51.2.
[19]Michael Polanyi, *Personal Knowledge: Toward a Post-Critical Philosophy* (New York: Harper & Row, 1962), p. 3.
[20]Ibid., p. 266.

Chapter 10: Head, Heart and Hands Together: Implications and Challenges

[1]Marva Dawn, *Reaching Out Without Dumbing Down: A Theology of Worship for the Turn-of-the-Century Culture* (Grand Rapids: Eerdmans, 1995), p. 4.
[2]Alan Jacobs, "Rhetoric and the Task of Apologetics in Contemporary America," *Proceedings of the Wheaton Theology Conference* 1 (1992): 169.
[3]Robert L. Wilken, "Religious Pluralism and Early Christian Thought," *Pro Ecclesia* 1, no. 1 (1992): 103.
[4]Dennis Hollinger, "The Church as Apologetic: A Sociology of Knowledge Perspective," in *Christian Apologetics in the Postmodern World*, ed. Timothy Phillips and Dennis Okholm (Downers Grove, Ill.: InterVarsity Press, 1995), p. 183. For further discussions about apologetics in the postmodern world, my chapter and the entire book may be helpful.
[5]Parker Palmer, *To Know as We Are Known: A Spirituality of Education* (San Francisco: Harper & Row, 1983), p. xii.
[6]Trudy Bush, interview with Dorothy Bass, "A Way to Live: The Shape of Christian Existence," *Christian Century*, February 24, 2004, p. 22.
[7]Miroslav Volf, "Theology for a Way of Life," in *Practicing Theology: Beliefs and Practices in Christian Life*, ed. Miroslav Volf and Dorothy Bass (Grand Rapids: Eerdmans, 2002), p. 249.
[8]Ibid., p. 260.

[9]M. Robert Mulholland Jr., *Invitation to a Journey: A Road Map for Spiritual Formation* (Downers Grove, Ill.: InterVarsity Press, 1993), p. 57.

[10]Ruth Benedict, *Patterns of Culture* (New York: Mentor Books, 1934), p. 72.

[11]Ibid., pp. 72-73.

[12]Mulholland, *Invitation,* p. 58.

[13]Ibid., p. 60.